An Owner's Guide to Male Midlife Crisis

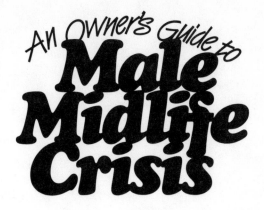

An Owner's Guide to
Male
Midlife
Crisis

Len D. McMillan

Pacific Press Publishing Association
Boise, Idaho
Montemorelos, Nuevo Leon, Mexico
Oshawa, Ontario, Canada

Edited by Don Mansell
Designed by Tim Larson
Cover Illustration by Donna Lang
Type set in 10/12 Century Schoolbook

Library of Congress Cataloging in Publication Data

McMillan, Len. D., 1938—
  Midstream without a paddle.

  1. Men—United States—Psychology. 2. Middle age—United
States—Psychological aspects. 3. Life change events—United States.
I. Title.
HQ1090.3.M386   1986   305.3'1   86-17070
ISBN 0-8163-0671-0

86 87 88 89 90 ● 5 4 3 2 1

Contents

A Midlife Profile

(Determining if you have the dread affliction!)

If you are between the ages of thirty-five and fifty put a check in front of the symptoms you can currently identify in your life. Remember, this applies to you *now* and not at some distant point in your past.

— I feel somewhat irrational at times and find it difficult to make a decision.

— I have an inner desire to change (job, spouse, education, etc.)

— I find myself fantasizing about what I would like to do if I wasn't tied down with kids and bills and house and car payments and a . . . !

— I feel that I have failed to achieve the goals I set for myself as a young man.

— I notice that some of the younger workers at my company are receiving promotions, and I am being passed over lately.

— I feel that I have missed out on much of what life has to offer. If I don't do something about it soon it will be too late.

— Sex has become very ho-hum lately. There seems to be little variety in my sex life. A key word is *boredom*.

— I seem to have trouble controlling my temper lately. Sometimes the slightest frustrations seem to set me off.

— My wife has noticed that I seem to complain a lot lately. I complain about the kids, my job, my back, my lack of . . . !

— I have noticed that I seem to have some bad moods that last for more than a few hours.

— Sometimes I awaken at 3:00 A.M. and find myself unable to go back to sleep.

— (If a Christian) I find myself becoming less and less interested in attending church and in regular Bible study.

— (If not a Christian) I find myself becoming more and more interested in what the Bible has to say about my life and my purpose for being on this earth.

— I seem to spend more and more time trying to comb my hair—even though there is less and less to comb.

— I seem to spend more time working late (or weekends) in order to keep up with my workload.

— I dread going to work each morning.

— I find myself bored and overeating. The most traveled path in our home is between the TV and the refrigerator.

— I find myself wanting to spend more and more time with "the boys" and less time at home.

— I have recently begun an intensive exercise program.

— I feel restless and useless without really understanding why.

— I find myself daydreaming more and more.

— A question that seems to bother me right now is, "Now what?"

— (If not a "teetotaler") I have begun to take a "little wine for my stomach's sake and often infirmities" in order to unwind after a hard day's work—even though I did not often drink wine (beer, alcohol) before.

— I have recently gotten a divorce.

— I find it necessary to get up frequently at night to pass water.

— I find myself waking at night bathed in sweat (hot or cold), and all sorts of anxieties flood my imagination.

— I have recently started taking blood-pressure medication.

— I have recently had to buy reading glasses.

— I have noticed a distinct bulge in my midriff when looking at my profile.

— I have recently purchased a new sports car.

— I have recently purchased a new wardrobe with a youthful emphasis.

— My daughter reminds me of my wife when we first started dating.

*Total up your check marks. If you have 20-30 you may be in a serious midlife crisis. If your total is 10-20 you may be approaching (or leaving) a midlife transition. If your total is 5-10 you may find it helpful to examine which particular statements you checked and question each one individually. If you checked less than 5 and you are over 40 years of age—you are indeed fortunate. *Congratulations!*

I Can't Believe This Is Happening to Me!

Have you ever woken up in the middle of the night and felt as if a thief was sneaking into your house? You distinctly remember locking the windows and bolting the doors, but this doesn't quiet your nervousness. Every board that creaks, every sighing of the wind outside raises your level of anxiety.

At first you are sure your ears are playing tricks on you, but then you hear what sounds like the muffled footfalls of a burglar. It's only my imagination working overtime, you say to yourself—only that and nothing more. You know your little castle is safe. You barred the gates and raised the drawbridge. So, ignoring the sounds, you try to go back to sleep.

But the footfalls persist, in fact they become more audible. No, you say to yourself, I'm not dreaming. . . . Suddenly you notice clusters of hair collecting at the bottom of the bathroom sink. Clusters that used to wave gently on your head now lie lifeless on the cold porcelain. You wash your face a second time and looking in the mirror, notice that your forehead has increased disproportionately to what it used to be. As you comb your hair you feel the comb sort of skip over an area near the back of your head. You notice that combing seems to require more skill, because you have to flip the hair "up and over" rather than straight back, like you used to do.

As you search your face in the mirror you continue to look for evidence of the dreaded blight of midlife. Do you really look any different today than you did yesterday? No! Emphatically, NO! you repeat to yourself. But what about last year? Wasn't there more hair on your head? Wasn't the hair a darker color? When did that bare spot appear on your scalp? How long have others noticed it? What! me getting bald. Oh NO! Not me. I'm too young for that to happen!

You're really beginning to feel anxious about now. Perhaps you need to wake up and take the Midlife Entrance Exam:

— 1. Do you remember the taste of Mom's cookies—but forget where you ate lunch yesterday?

— 2. Do you recognize more names in the obituaries than in the box scores?

— 3. Do you still care about the whales—but identify more with Jonah?

— 4. When your wife suggests a massage, do you take off your shoes?

— 5. Do you find yourself squaring your shoulders and holding in your stomach whenever you are in the presence of others?

— 6. Did you finally give up the notion of becoming president of the nation, the company, or the Cub Scouts?

— 7. Do you find yourself thinking more about sex—but enjoying it less?

If you answered these questions positively, you can be sure the thief *has* crept into your house.

As one author suggests, one has entered midlife when he finds himself preoccupied with such matters as health, success, and sexual potency. Along with this he may experience a loss of interest in his work and a loss of faith in his abilities. He may find it hard to concentrate and make decisions, may become cranky and bored or irritated with his spouse—may even lust after extramarital affairs.[1]

Those afflicted with the midlife malady know it is a time of confusion, urgency, fear, insecurity, depression, boredom, anger, and identity crisis all rolled up in one shivering mass of humanity.

The crisis precipitating this phenomenon may come in many forms, but they all begin with the same word: *LOSS*—loss of looks, loss of youth, loss of health, loss of fertility, loss of libido, loss of religious beliefs, loss of marital commitment, loss of promotions, loss of creativity, loss of poise, loss of personality— loss, *Loss, LOSS!*

Edmund Bergler refers to the midlife crisis as "the revolt of the middle-aged man." For some men it is a time of introspection. As they look back over their lives they realize they have been molded by everyone along the way—from their mothers, teachers, wives, companies, policies, vocational expectations— until they literally do not know who they are.

When a man finally feels he has given the basics to his wife and family, he often feels betrayed or even rejected because in so doing he has missed so much himself. He has missed the new cars, new clothes, time off, and long vacations. Filled with frustration and uncontrolled emotions, he reaches out for everything he thinks he has missed. However, these symbols of his rebellion are merely the outward expression of an inner frustration that has been present for some time—a deep sense of depersonalization.

I have felt most of these feelings myself. My wife used to good-naturedly poke fun at me because I bought an old 1957 Chevy convertible and restored it at the age of forty. I could not afford one when they were new, yet I had always wanted to own this classic automobile. To be honest I suppose I actually enjoyed it more at midlife than I would have in my teens. Somehow it helped me realize a dream and boost my drooping self-image at the same time. Often, when I was feeling depressed, I would go out to the garage, back the car out on the driveway, put down the top, turn on the radio, and just sit there for twenty or thirty minutes. If that therapy didn't work, I would go for a short drive and enjoy watching the passersby waving and pointing at my car. It never failed to lift my spirits. Of course, it didn't help me regain my lost youth, but it helped anyway.

One of the major factors contributing to the midlife crisis is the realization that time flies and that much of it has already passed you by. You have lived more than half of your life. It is like being at the top of a mountain, and all that lies ahead is downhill. Everything from that moment on seems to be anticlimatic as you realize that you have passed the peak of your experience. Whether that is actually true or not is immaterial to the midlife male. He feels that it is true, and that is enough. As Roger Gould has put it, "The desire for stability and continuity which characterized our thirties is being replaced by a relentless inner demand for action. The sense of timelessness in our early thirties is giving way to an awareness of the pressure of time in our forties. *Whatever we must do must be done now!*"[2]

Middle age actually intensifies all the difficulties we thought would go away someday. Difficulties in our own behavior or that of our spouse. Difficulties with our job or our children. All these problems are still there at midlife, waiting for us, bigger and bolder than ever.

Oftentimes the problems are actually a more intense repetition of problems we've always lived with. But, now we can no longer stand them nor expect them to go away. A sense of frustration overtakes us as we recognize the finality of it all. This realization brings about new tensions based upon old problems that have never been resolved. But, believe it or not, such tensions can actually lead to real growth and change. If they do not, they can cause us to fall in despair.

When the midlife crisis hits a man, his closest ally may be an understanding wife and a strong marriage. Yet, at this time in his life he is liable to have neither. His wife may not realize that he is struggling—or she may not care, because of her own problems. He may find it difficult to explain to her. Their communication may have become focused on running the family, not explaining the depths of his soul. They no longer exchange ideas or talk about their feelings. Their sexual relationship may have become almost nonexistent because they are usually tired or busy. Not only do they find their married life dull and boring, but if there are tensions between them these can become almost unbearable.

A midlife male has a special brand of insecurity not known to others. He sees change taking place so rapidly in today's society that his skills have become obsolete. Most companies today find it easier to hire a young man or woman fresh out of college to run the computers than to retool an old brain that has so much to unlearn. Job security is, in fact, a real crisis for the midlife male. He used to feel confident and perhaps even "cocky" about his abilities. Now he realizes that some may classify him as obsolete—along with the equipment he was trained to work with.

As he looks back over his life, the midlife male may even feel cheated that he was forced to work at a job he didn't really enjoy. One father reminded his son (with a trace of bitterness in his voice), "Why do you think you're entitled to find work that makes you happy? I made it by the rules of the game, why can't you? I worked all my life in a mundane, routine job that I simply endured in order to give the family security."[3]

A major emotion frequently manifest in the midlife male is *anger*. In fact he may display various stages of the anger process most of the time. He is angry because he is growing old, angry because he feels tired, angry because of financial obligations, angry that he has not reached his career goals (or if he has, it hasn't made any difference), angry that people don't understand him, angry that the kids only want him for the things he provides, not who he is, angry that no one seems to appreciate him, angry that life is such a big waste of time, angry that God has let his life be this way—angry, *Angry,* **ANGRY!**

When the midlife male becomes angry with himself he may just sit for hours, depressed with all these negative emotions churning inside. Self-pity ranks high on his list of feelings along with self-judgments that constantly eat away at his self-confidence. One thing is certain—*self* has become the center of his being. As he turns his anger inward, depression becomes more and more evident, and, the sad thing is that he will eventually lose his self-confidence which has seen him through all the previous crises in his life.

When all of these feelings of frustration and insecurity are combined with a general feeling of the uselessness of life, you have the picture of the midlife male drowning in a sea of intense feelings and helplessness. These feelings tend to become self-feeding. The more helpless he feels himself to be, the more helpless he becomes. The more helpless he becomes, the more evident his feelings, which only verify his own feeling of inadequacy.

To break this vicious cycle of depression requires strong positive action on the part of the midlife male and those around him. He must begin to act on the basis of his own personal worth—as measured by the value God places upon him. As he regains his sense of self-worth, he is enabled once again to find his role in life. By understanding what is happening to him, he can begin to chip away at the painful, destructive feelings of depression.

Dr. Edgar Jackson, in his book *Coping With the Crises in Your Life,* recommends positive action in three areas to reverse the progressive nature of depression:[4]

> **Physical:** "At the physical level we can exercise the large muscle system until the blood flows freely, purifying itself and stimulating glandular and visceral activity. This restoration of a more healthful function of physical organs aids in restoring intrapsychic balance."
>
> **Emotional:** "At the emotional level we can stop passing destructive judgments upon ourselves and begin to accept the universe and the people in it as if they had a right to be themselves rather than projections of our own way of looking at things."
>
> **Intellectual:** At the intellectual level "we can set some goals for our growth into a new and more adequate philosophy of life that can stimulate our development and our next step into maturity."

The problem with depression and that other midlife symptom—boredom—is that each is essentially a vacuum. A bored person is one whose life has become empty. Similarly, a depressed person is one who has forced everything of value out of his life and is likewise empty. But as the saying goes, nature abhors a vacuum, and sooner or later something is bound to rush in to fill the void, and thus change can be good or bad.

Change is a vital ingredient in the midlife male's attempt to cope with these strange feelings and forces in his life. Unfortunately, the initial changes are frequently negative, and the midlife male's reactions to them can make it difficult (if not impossible) to understand his strange behavior. Thus he may seem to have some deep-seated compulsion to change everything in his life. But these changes are as futile as attempting to delay the inevitable. The simple fact is, such a person is growing older.

Sally Conway, the wife of a man who went through a dramatic midlife crisis and author of *You and Your Husband's Midlife Crisis,* offers this helpful description of the typical midlife male undergoing changes in his life:[5]

> Grouchiness and sharp words often replace his customary kindness and gentleness. Restlessness and vacillation erode his usual stable composure. Instead of exuding an air of confidence and boldness, he often seems anxious and insecure. Sometimes he wants to be babied; at other times he demands to be left alone. He is aloof and uncommunicating, or he lashes out irrationally at everyone and everything. He wears an air of martyrdom.
>
> Formerly optimistic and challenged when difficulties came along, he now sits depressed and immobilized by self-pity. He sometimes lets obligations slip by without meeting them as he did faithfully for years. He finds excuses for not spending time with you or the children and shuns social activities at every opportunity. Perhaps he has resigned his leadership positions in the church, attends the services less frequently or not at all now, and sometimes voices profane complaints against God that greatly disturb you.
>
> These changes in your mid-life husband are symptoms of a struggle going on inside him.

References

1. Robert Lee and Marjorie Casebier, *The Spouse Gap: Weathering the Marriage Crisis During Middlescence* (Nashville, Tenn.: Abingdon Press, 1971), p. 62.

2. Roger L. Gould, *Transformations: Growth and Change in Adult Life* (New York: Simon and Schuster, 1978), p. 217.

3. Lee, p. 78.

4. Edgar N. Jackson, *Coping With the Crises in Your Life* (New York: Jason Aronson, 1980), p. 133.

5. Sally Conway, *You and Your Husband's Mid-Life Crisis* (Elgin, Ill.: David C. Cook Publishing Co., 1980), pp. 16, 17.

Midlife: A Definition

In her 1976 bestseller *Passages,* Gail Sheehy gave Americans a new way of looking at themselves. She popularized a fresh psychological theory of the way adults develop, change, and grow. Grown-ups, she maintained, must pass through a set series of age-linked periods which she called "predictable crises of adult life."

One of the primary sources of her book was Daniel J. Levinson, professor of psychology at Yale University and author of *The Seasons of a Man's Life.* From his studies of the lives of middle-aged American men, Levinson concluded that every man passes through an orderly sequence of psychosocial periods, none lasting more than seven to ten years. During each period of time a man is faced with specific tasks, choices, and problems. Stable periods, during which these problems are temporarily resolved, alternate with transitional periods, during which new concerns, challenges, or opportunities for change arise.

One stage that caught the public eye was his "mid-life transition" through which a man passes sometime between the ages of forty and forty-five. It is in this stage, says Levinson, that a man begins to assess how well he has succeeded in reaching the goals he set for himself in his twenties. During this period of midlife passage, many men struggle to find new meaning in their lives. Levinson is quick to clarify that the age categories are rather inexact since many "influences" along the way shape and mold a person's life. These influences may speed or slow down the process, or even produce alternate routes or detours along the way. In some extreme cases, he conclude, the developmental process may stop altogether.

The research used in Levinson's book shows that up to 80 percent of American men suffer moderate to severe symptoms in making the midlife transition. This is understandable in our modern society since we have become a "people on the move." This mobility has deprived us of the roots and stability enjoyed by previous generations. Most of us no longer live in the place of our birth. For many, we are no longer supported by the extended family (because they now extend all across the country) or even live close to our immediate family. When a crisis comes our way, we play the "game" alone. Most of the time we are afraid to admit we are even experiencing any difficulty—let alone a crisis. This is particularly true for the "macho" male.

To further complicate matters, machines and computers have depersonalized many aspects of our lives. We no longer correspond with an individual at our bank but with a computer. Our credit rating no longer depends on a personal interview but upon the whims of a computer. It seems that computers separate us from the person we thought we were—until now, at midlife, we are not certain that person ever existed. We live in an age of knowledge explosion. If we have been out of school more than five years, our knowledge is "out of date." Never before in history has the midlife male been such a victim of a "world economy" that rudely pushes him out of his comfortable nest of isolation.

The midlife individual (male or female) may discover that even though he or she makes up only one fourth of the U.S. population, he or she makes three fourths of the decisions and pays three fourths of the nation's debt. This places tremendous pressure upon those going through a midlife crisis. It is important to remember that midlife is a relatively new experience for much of the world's population. Life expectancy during the Bronze Age averaged only eighteen. At the height of the Greek civilization it rose to twenty. During the Middle Ages the life expectancy was thirty-one. In the nineteenth century here in the U.S. it was only thirty-seven. Now our life expectancy is approaching eighty. With more and more males living to experience midlife, the symptoms have become easier to recognize and define.

Because "midlife" is a rather recent discovery in psychological circles, some have questioned whether there really is such a thing as the midlife crisis. In his book *God Invented Sex,* Dr. Charles Wittschiebe quotes a letter that appeared in *Medical Economics:*[1]

> Dear Mr. Editor:
> The "male menopause" syndrome—if it is that—seems to have hit our entire area, and divorces and separations are rampant in the 40-50 age range. My physician-husband is one of these men who is very disturbed, has lost all sexual interest in me, lost interest in the practice, feels that marriage is outmoded, and contradicts himself constantly in statements. I spoke to two psychiatrists about this—one said to leave, another refused to help because there is no way to force my husband to seek help when he refuses. He admits he needs psychiatric help but will see no one.
>
> We are prominent in our area. Our children are intelligent—two teen-agers and one younger, with a great deal of schooling ahead of them. And my husband is proud to escort me to various functions, as I present a good appearance and have kept up with his interests.
>
> We have a good marriage—or had one—and I fear we will be another statistic in the growing rate of divorce in the medical community of our area.
>
> Please help with an article on this problem. Thank you.
> Another medical wife.
> P.S. I love my husband deeply.

The editors of *Medical Economics* then asked a number of female and male consultants—chiefly doctors and doctors' wives—to comment on the letter and the resulting article that was written before it went to publication. To the editors' surprise the readers agreed that male menopause was indeed increasing and that it is usually the wife who is blamed, if his menopausal state is more than a "reluctant farewell to youth."

Sometimes those things that are most painful to us are best examined through the use of humor. Just what is male menopause—middlescence—or midlife crisis? Perhaps the following quotes may give us a starting point for our search:

"Middle age is when your age starts to show around your middle."—Bob Hope.

"Middle age is when anything new in the way you feel is most likely a symptom."—Laurence Peter.

"You know you've reached middle age when your weight lifting consists of standing up."—Bob Hope.

"Middle age is when your clothes no longer fit, and it's you who needs the alteration."—Earl Wilson.

"You know you're getting older when the candles cost more than the cake."—Bob Hope.

It is often therapeutic for us to laugh at our crises. This can help us gain a proper perspective of ourselves. When we are no longer able to laugh at a predicament, it is an indication that the temporary stimulus of humor cannot meet the deep-seated needs we are experiencing. Therefore, for some reading this book, the following quotes will be more to the point:

"The awareness that time is finite is a particularly conspicuous feature of middle-age.

Life is restructured in terms of the time-left-to-live rather than time-since-birth."—Bernice L. Neugarten, Ph.D.

"No one believes in his own death. . . . In the unconscious everyone is convinced of his own immortality."—Sigmund Freud.

"The real voyage of discovery consists not in seeking new landscapes, but in having new eyes."—Marcel Proust.

"I don't believe one grows older. I think that what happens early on in life is that at a certain age one stands still and stagnates."—T. S. Eliot.

"We cannot live the afternoon of life according to the program of life's morning; for what was great in the morning will be little in the evening, and what in the morning was true will at evening become a lie."—Carl Jung.

"Of all the barbarous middle ages, that which is most barbarous is the middle age of man; it is—I really scarce know what; but when we hover between fool and sage."—Byron.

Some have referred to midlife as a second adolescence. In many ways this is true. Psychologically things happen to you in much the same manner as during your first adolescence. You begin to have mood swings. People, even close friends, cannot figure out why you are acting so strangely. Sometimes you are antisocial and even rude. You seem to have an identity crisis. But, unlike your first adolescence, this crisis becomes more of an inquest than a quest. The long, hard look you take at your life may leave a bad taste in your mouth.

One major difference between your second and first adolescence is that a person in his forties usually cannot run away from life like a person in his teens. Usually the midlife male is locked into many responsibilities and he feels trapped. Like an animal caught in a trap, he doesn't know whether to stay and be killed by the hunter or chew off his foot and go through the rest of his life maimed. Either way he loses.

It is a sad commentary on life that we seem to spend one-fourth of our lives growing up and three fourths growing old. The midlife transition is intertwined with all of one's former (and future) life. Everything a person has done and thought in the past and everything he will do and think and become in the future is all a part of the midlife crisis. Yet the one fourth of our life spent growing up is seen as the ultimate age by many midlife males. This belief is fostered by the mass media's emphasis on youth. The present generation is caught up in the transition from a parent-oriented society to a youth-oriented one. Youth has become the key to current advertizing and only adds fuel to the fire of insecurity already burning within the midlife male.

Have you noticed that in current advertising—

Teenagers always seem to have bright, glistening (and straight) teeth, while adults have dentures and bad breath?

Young people have fun at amusement parks and beach parties, while older people watch TV—get nagging headaches, and upset stomachs?

The youthful wife makes a cup of coffee that turns her husband into a sex maniac, but the middle-aged wife spends all day washing, mopping, and ironing only to have her husband come home tired and cross with aching muscles, hay fever, allergies, and a headache with Excedrin written all over it?

Young people wear sneakers and sandals, have fun, and laugh even with their mouth full of hair, but older people wear support hose and girdles, have constipation, pyorrhea, tired blood, and insomnia?

If the current emphasis on youthfulness continues, the next generation may go through their midlife crisis at the age of thirty. Because of our intense focus on youth, the middle-aged male finds his work and social life hopelessly intertwined. Employers do not wish to hire him if he is past forty-five. Even though recent statistics indicate the average employment period is less than six years, many employers are brainwashed by the media into thinking a young person offers them the best future and will stay with the company the rest of his life. The facts are otherwise. Young people seldom stay with the company they began with, but use their first three or four jobs as steppingstones to something better.

Combining the influence of the media with the rejection of employers causes the midlife male to conclude that if anything of value is going to happen in his career, it must happen before the age of forty-five. Thus, he begins to feel depressed, loses his self-confidence, and withdraws from friends and society if that goal has not been achieved.

It is at this time that he begins to seriously consider the possibility of death. He has been so busy growing up that he never really paid much attention to death before. His formative years were so full of change·that there was no time for death. Establishing a marriage and a career kept him preoccupied during his twenties and thirties. But now death suddenly becomes a reality. Men he went to school with are dying from heart attacks and cancer. His own parents may be ill or dying. He realizes there is more of life behind him than ahead of him.

Feeling depressed, he determines to increase the physical activity in his life. However, he finds he can no longer sink his hook shot or even touch the rim. His hundred-yard dash has now become more of an occasional jog. A game of touch football requires three days of recuperation. Not only is he mortal, but he is losing his physical prowess. For the man whose self-image is based on his physical abilities, this can be devastating.

As the midlife male struggles with his self-image and reviews his past, he inevitably reaches one of four conclusions about his life:[2]

1. **He Is a Failure.** He may try to escape his own conclusions through alcohol, drugs, work, suicide, or a protective stoicism, which accepts the fact that "that is just the way it is."

2. **The Results Are Inconclusive.** This is the most common adjustment made by the midlife male, since it enables him to keep on in the hope that something will eventually turn up.

3. **He Has Been Partially Successful.** This provides him with the best chance of achieving happiness, giving him a sense of fulfillment while helping him modify goals that were too high.

4. **He Has Been Successful.** Though ideally the man who arrives at this conclusion should be happiest, such is rarely the case. Usually the successful man tends to feel dissatisfied with the goals he chose or with the road he took that brought him to where he is.

Midlife is a time of intense soul-searching, review, reevaluation—a time of adjustment, acceptance, and accommodation. It is a time to become familiar with the Bible, especially the books of Psalms and Ecclesiastes. Many of the Bible poets had appropriate comments to make concerning the midlife crisis. One psalmist even mentions midlife when he laments, "He has broken my strength in mid-course; he has shortened my days. 'O my God,' I say, 'take me not hence in the midst of my days, thou whose years endure throughout all generations!' " Psalm 102:23, 24, RSV.

Robert Raines summarizes the midlife crisis succinctly in his poem "Lord, Could You Make It a Little Better?"

> Middle-agers are beautiful!
>   aren't we, Lord?
> I feel for us
>   too radical for our parents
>   too reactionary for our kids
>   supposedly in the prime of life
>   like prime rib
>   everybody eating off me
>   devouring me
>   nobody thanking me
>   appreciating me
>   but still hanging in there
>   communicating with my parents
>   in touch with my kids
>   and getting more in touch with myself
> and that's all good
>   thanks for making it good,
> and—
>   could you make it a little better?

References

1. Charles E. Wittschiebe, *God Invented Sex* (Nashville, Tenn: Southern Publishing Association, 1974), pp. 75-77.
2. Lee, p. 76.

Stages of Midlife

It is a curious fact that the basic stages of a midlife crisis closely parallel those of the grief process following the death of a loved one. The first stage is *denial*—this can't really be happening to me. Surely it is only a dream or, at worst, a nightmare! It cannot be so! I'm not getting old. There hasn't been that much of a change in my physical appearance—since yesterday.

Denial seems to calm the troubled waters of the midlife mind for a short time. The midlife male may even be able to continue on as though nothing is happening for a few weeks, months, or sometimes years. Inevitably, however, the bathroom mirror (and every other reflective surface) confirms the fact that he *is* getting older. It no longer helps to replace all the hundred-watt bulbs with forty watters because he can still see the lines in his time-etched face even with limited lighting.

This leads to the second stage of the midlife crisis—*anger*. When the truth finally begins to dawn on him, he becomes angry. He may delay the outburst for a time by standing some distance from the mirror, and musing that, like a fine painting, he looks much better from a distance—the farther away the better.

He begins to feel an inner anger, perhaps even rage. "Why me? It's not really fair. Why me? Why must I be born into a youth-oriented society? Why me? Why am I prematurely turning gray and losing my hair? Why me?"

At this stage it is almost impossible for him to react rationally due to the anger churning inside him. He finds it increasingly difficult to talk about his feelings with friends or even his spouse. How does he explain to someone that he is angry because the natural process of aging is taking place in his body?

Even though he doesn't really want to talk about it, friends need to be attentive to what is happening inside of him. If they tell him not to feel angry, he immediately feels they don't understand. This only reinforces his anger and drives it deeper inside. What he really needs is a listening ear, not a vocalized conscience.

The third stage of midlife is *bargaining*. He begins to bargain with himself, his mate—even God. Maybe, he reasons, he can replay his youth once more before it is too late. Perhaps he can buy and restore that 1957 Chevy convertible he couldn't afford as a teenager. Maybe by going on a diet and exercising regularly he can reclaim his body. Perhaps by contacting a hairpiece manufacturer or rubbing on monoxidil salve, he can even reclaim his lost hair. Maybe, given a little more time, he can become a success in his chosen career. He may even rationalize that by having a brief affair he can restore the sexual vitality that seems to be ebbing away.

For the bargaining midlife male, the message still comes through loud and clear: "Your life is now half over. In fact, you are on the downward side." The midlife male has a lot to look back on, and ideally, a lot to look forward to. He begins to realize that life is a very brief voyage at best. He may even begin to wonder if life has any meaning beyond the endless need to survive.

Also, at some point in midlife, he comes to the realization that he knows more dead people than living ones. The truth becomes all too apparent. What is happening to him is real because it is also happening to his friends. His bargaining has not delayed at all the aging process.

At this point the midlife male slips silently and steadily into the fourth stage—*depression*. Alas, all is lost! He realizes he cannot regain his lost youth. There is no way to stop the aging process. He may succeed in covering it up for a season, but it is a delaying game at best. When that realization finally sinks in, he begins to withdraw into his secret shell. He withdraws from friends, from social functions, from family—even from his wife. Life is now at its lowest ebb.

He may even begin to see death as a kind of escape hatch from reality. A leap off a bridge would silence all the mouths of his creditors, mockers, competitors, family, and even his own self-depreciation. One author comments, "I have never been convinced that the act of suicide is anything else but the final expression of a subtle psychotic process that began as an option and grew into a powerful force that seduced the person's mind."[1]

I don't know if you have ever walked through a long tunnel and stopped to assess your progress about half way through. I once walked through a mile-long railroad tunnel in Wisconsin. As long as I was walking and looking straight ahead it didn't bother me. But, about half way through the tunnel I stopped and looked back. For a moment panic set in as I saw only pinpoints of light no matter which way I looked—forward or backward. I wondered if I would ever get out of this tunnel. From the vantage point of the middle, it seemed a hopeless task. The midlife male goes through a similar experience. No matter which way he looks, there seems to be no way out of the situation.

During this time of depression, a man may try to cope with the reality of his own death. Even though it may lie many years in the future, it seems close at hand. As he ponders the future, the midlife male chooses one of four options concerning death:[2]

1. He may *deny* that he is going to die because death is linked with old age, and, if he is still trying to deny the aging process, he will find it difficult to accept the reality of death for him.
2. He may accept *defeat* becoming so discouraged by the reality of his ultimate death that he gives up his desire to continue living.
3. He may find himself overcome with the *fear* of death. This oppressive fear may be the result of feeling

unprepared to face the judgment of a righteous God
and its consequences if he is condemned.
4. *Acceptance* of death is the final possibility. It takes
many forms. Some accept it grudgingly—like W. C.
Fields who had these words engraved on his tomb-
stone: "I'd rather be in Philadelphia."

The final stage in the midlife crisis is *acceptance* of the aging
process. The wise midlife male finally comes to terms with the
aging process and can say, "All right! I can handle this! It's OK.
In fact, I'm looking forward to this new adventure in my life."
Acceptance is usually a process that occurs over a period of
time, as he accepts himself more and more just as he is.

If a midlife male does not pass through all five stages, he may
get hung up on one stage and suffer their unpleasant symptoms
for months or even years. Like the adolescent who never ma-
tures to adulthood, the midlife male who never resolves his
problems may linger in one stage or another indefinitely.
Sometimes a man delays his acceptance of midlife until he gets
into his late fifties. Some men never accept it at all. Such men
become more and more noticeable in a crowd. Their dress and
manner seem out of place for their age. They are still trying to
maintain a youthful lifestyle when they should be accepting
the fact that such attempts are futile and perhaps even more
damaging to their self-image than accepting the truth about
themselves. Acceptance provides the final key to unlocking a
frustrating experience in the life of most midlife males.

References

1. David C. Morley, *Halfway Up the Mountain* (Old Tappan, N.J.:
Fleming H. Revell Co., 1979), p. 74.
2. Jim Conway, *Men in Mid-Life Crisis* (Elgin, Ill.: David C. Cook
Publishing Co., 1978), pp. 268, 269.

Unwilling Victim or Subconscious Accomplice?

"Experience is not what happens to a man. It is what a man does with what happens to him."—Aldous Huxley.

"You don't have to suffer continual chaos in order to grow."—John C. Lilly.

"The only things worth learning are the things you learn after you know it all."—Harry S. Truman.

"Life does not need to be changed. Only our attitudes do."—Sri Swami Rama.

Although there is a lot of talk these days about stress, especially the stress of midlife, not all stress is bad. When stress is positive, we call it a "challenge." But when stress is negative, we call it a "crisis." Actually, whether or not a situation is stressful depends more on the individual then the situation. One person's crisis may be another person's challenge.

For some men (approximately 20 percent), a midlife crisis never occurs. That may be partly due to their temperament type, but it is also the result of how they view themselves. In midlife, something inside forces the male to examine himself, his society, and his lifestyle. He begins to suspect that the goals he set for himself as a young man may never be realized, if he continues to obey the rules he was taught in childhood.

"The resultant slow splintering or fast fracture of personality can resemble a hellish game that seems to be played in an endless pit of snakes with no ladders. The snakes are self-doubt, self-loathing, and self-destruction and the rest of the family will find them very difficult to put up with."[1]

33

This period evokes tumultuous struggles within the self, and even with the external world. Every aspect of the midlife male's life now comes into question, and he may be horrified by what he sees. He is filled with recriminations against himself and others. He feels that he cannot continue as before. The old values he grew up believing just are not working. He needs time and space to choose either a new path or drastically modify the old one. During this period when he is facing his greatest uncertainties, other events may happen to influence the increasing change in his personality. He may face such crises as bankruptcy, job loss, divorce, death of a loved one, or a myriad of other possibilities.

The doubting, uncertainty, and searching apparent at this time is reality to most midlife males. But the vital question is: How best can he cope with them? Anyone who has been through such a period knows that you usually stumble out of the stage a better person. A successful midlife crisis can actually make you a better person. It can increase your self-awareness, self-sufficiency, independence, contentment, and, above all, your faith and confidence in God's plan for your life. The alternative is a male trying to perpetuate youth and denying reality until the day he dies, and in the process incurring unnecessary expense in terms of money, spirit, and even shame.

Only a few get through life without some sort of identity crisis. These crises do not necessarily occur during midlife. Whenever an identity crisis strikes, it has usually been lurking in the shadows for some time. A person may wake up some morning and wonder What is the point of going on? What is the point of going to work? Or, such a crisis may creep up silently and unexpected as a slow realization of futility.

David Morley describes the final assault on the mountain of life in a midlife crisis in this manner:

> From here on to the peak, the climb will be steeper. The warmth of the base of the mountain is replaced by a creeping invasion of cold. He is moving further and further away from the vibrant focus of youth that made him feel so secure in his humanness. Now the pace slackens. The

rocks have little green upon them and here and there are patches of ice. His feet begin to slip. Time moves more slowly. The conditions all demand a change of pace—a new technique of climbing to deal with the change in conditions.[2]

Some men going through the midlife crisis have been living for others for many years. This is especially true of those who have been reared in a Christian environment. Such individuals have been taught to deny their own desires in order to meet the needs of others—their families and their friends; and even strangers. It is the need to support the family that gets them up each morning when the alarm rings. They have willingly accepted increasing responsibility at work, in the community, in their church, and of course, in their family.

By the time such a person has reached midlife, he is not only getting physically tired, but he is getting emotionally drained as well. As he looks about for relief, he sees he is tied to his obligations by unbreakable chains of need and guilt. He cannot escape, even for a little while. So many people are demanding so much. To make matters even worse, his own male ego will not let him admit he can no longer carry the load. He begins to get sick and tired of it all, and the need to escape becomes compulsive. After all the years of serving others (for whatever reasons), the midlife male experiencing a crisis feels that he is ready to serve himself for a change. "After all," he reasons, "Don't I deserve it? It's time to do things *my* way!" But is such a response the response of a mature adult, or an immature adolescent?

In some ways it seems that our society rewards individuals who act in an immature manner. We applaud the man who breaks out of the "chains" that bind him. Never mind that in so doing he may be destroying other lives. Never mind that his marriage may break up. Never mind that the children may be scarred for life. Never mind that his employer is paying him good wages to act like a responsible adult. The middle-age male who leaves his job and his family and takes off with his twenty-year-old secretary is not considered a fool—but a folk hero by many. Never mind the tragic consequences and broken lives he leaves behind. He is considered a real champion because he had the courage to *do it his way!*

But, not all midlife males are self-centered enough to do it *their way*. For some it is a continuing dilemma. If the male facing a midlife crisis runs to escape the pressures facing him in life, his conscience plagues him; if he tries to stay and fight the "dragons" on his own, depression consumes him. Of all the stages and transitions a man goes through in adulthood, the midlife crisis is potentially the most dangerous and usually the most painful for him, his family, his employer, and his church.

One man described the dilemma of the midlife male with these words: "One of the hardest things for me has been to watch my wife choke back tears, trying to be strong and carry the responsibility of the family, at the same time trying to be optimistic, happy, and support me. Part of me would say, 'That's not fair that she has to carry this load,' but the other part of me would say, 'I'm sorry; I can't do anything about it.' "[3]

It can be extremely difficult to live with a man who is going through the midlife transition. One day he may act like an immature adolescent, with tremendous outbursts of anger or deep depression and withdrawal; the next he may appear perfectly normal and you wonder if he is the same person. The average midlife male frequently presents a picture of instability and uncertainty. He doesn't know who he is, where he is going, or what he is doing. His values are as confused as his current goals in life.

This transition period normally brings with it all the accompanying feelings of grief, pressure, and anxiety, to name a few. For some the crisis is evidenced by floundering behavior. For others it is more quiet (yet just as painful) and not nearly as devastating to those around them. It is a time in one's life when important decisions must be made. Unfortunately, it may be the worst possible time to make such life-changing decisions. Each decision becomes a "hinge-point" for the rest of his life. The real difficulty may not always be in making the decisions (these may come too easily), but in living with the regrets later.

Many midlife males are so filled with anxiety and apprehension over the aging process that their entire personalities change. One who has been quiet and unassuming suddenly becomes outspoken and brash. One who has been able to make instant decisions is unable to decide what color shirt to wear. He may become a living denial of himself as he tries to rip away the masks and find out who he really is. Not all men enter into such drastic confrontations, of course. For some, it is like weaving a cocoon from which they later emerge as a new and altogether lovely creation.

In a man's first adolescence there is a struggle to find a personality of his own, strong and independent from his parents. During the second adolescence there is a need to discover meaning in life—significant enough to last all the rest of his days. The midlife male has lived enough of his life to know who he is and to actually test the authenticity of his basic understanding against life itself. Now he has a deeper question to answer: "Why am I here, and what difference will it make when I'm gone?" The answer emerging from this intense inner struggle will determine whether the crisis of his midlife years is a beginning or an end to his personal growth. Either he grows into a full mature human being, or he finds other psychological "handles" on which to hang his identity crisis.

From this intense struggle there may emerge a healthy, happy human being—or an individual unable to cope with life. There are three basic classifications of psychological behavior defined as "unhealthy" responses to the midlife crisis:[4]

1. Character Disorders: Such disorders usually have their roots early in life. Normal development in communication and relationship is thwarted, and the child retreats into his inner being. Because his capacity for normal feelings has never been fully developed, he is usually unable to fully perceive the feelings of others. He tends to manipulate and use others rather than respond normally to them.

This type of character disorder is usually the result of a personal crisis early in life. But this isn't all. This disorder has a tendency to produce crises in the lives of others. Women who marry men with this kind of disorder are likely to suffer throughout their married life. Normal people expect normal responses, but people with character disorders apparently are incapable of responding normally.

When a person with this type of disorder approaches midlife and experiences an identity crisis the results can be devastating to him as well as to those around him. The failure of such people to know who they are tends to prevent them from working through the crisis. As a result they tend to progress to one of the next two stages.

2. Neurotic Behavior: The person who suffers from a neurosis feels excessive anxiety much of the time. When he no longer can cope with the anxiety in his usual forms of action, he retreats into earlier types of problem-solving behavior. Instead of solving his problem it makes it worse, because his response is basically immature and often inappropriate. People usually accept a tantrum by a three-year-old as normal behavior due to the child's immaturity, but the same tantrum exhibited by a forty-three-year-old is unacceptable and frequently precipitates a crisis. Neurotics tend to be obsessive-compulsives and frequently overdo or exaggerate everything from drinking to symptoms of illness. A neurotic may even turn his anxieties into paralyzing physical symptoms in an attempt to escape stress.

The neurotic's response to a crisis usually has the effect of projecting his problems onto others, whether it be his family, his work place, his church, or his school. Such persons tend to export their inner conflicts, making others irritable, suspicious, and disturbed. Neurotics seem to have a knack of setting people against people, as if increasing the crisis in the lives of others can somehow reduce their own stress. Such behavior tends to boomerang and, in effect, increases the neurotic's stress, setting up a kind of vicious cycle. Thus, neuroses can be quite uncomfortable, both for the neurotic and those around him. But, neuroses can be treated.

3. Psychotic Behavior: The psychotic is a person who has snapped under stress and cannot cope with it in the normal process of living. While the neurotic may continue to work (while making himself and those around him miserable), the psychotic tends to lose touch with reality and may be unable to work or even continue living with his family. It is common for psychotics to become so suspicious that they are afraid to eat because they think their food has been poisoned, or they may find the real world so intolerable that they retreat into an unreal world, where they feel "safe" and "comfortable." But this "safe house" is so out of correspondence with reality that it produces a nonconformity pattern that is difficult if not impossible for others to live with.

While the neurotic knows that something is wrong, the psychotic usually is unaware of his true condition. He may think he is the only one who sees things as they really are and may consider that everyone else is disturbed. The emotional life of the psychotic is one of extreme reaction. He may, for instance, show little or no emotional response to pain or crises, or he may fly into a rage and shout over some insignificant occurrence.

Psychotics are difficult to treat, but their cases are not entirely hopeless. Improved methods of care now make it possible for many psychotics to return to a more normal way of life under professional supervision.

Fortunately most people do not fit into the category of psychotics. Furthermore, it is well to remember that most midlife crises are temporary, and the individuals involved usually graduate with "honors" in a few months or years.

References

1. Shirley Conran, *Futures: How to Survive Life After Thirty* (London: Sidgwick and Jackson, 1979), p. 58.
2. Morley, p. 39.
3. Jim Conway, p. 157.
4. Jackson, pp. 73-75.

My Body: Public Enemy Number One!

Imagine the scene. You are at the beach with your wife. As you sit under your umbrella you cannot help but notice the lean physiques of the younger men in their late teens and early twenties. What a difference between their abdominal "concavity" and your flabby, abominable "convexity."

As you rise to your feet you self-consciously "suck up your guts"—like they taught you in the army years ago. You're doing your best to put on a good "front." But looking down (trying to be casual, of course), you notice a slight outward bulge in your abdomen. You tighten your muscles even more and square your shoulders. However, when you start walking toward the water, you quickly realize that your unnatural gait resembles more that of an ape than an olympic athlete. As you meditate on your physical condition, you relax, and when next you survey your anatomy you observe that your ample waist is again hanging over your swimming trunks.

From that day on you begin to be very conscious of pulling in your stomach. Not infrequently you catch your reflection in a mirror or a store window and—oops! your "chest" has slipped. You also remember the not-so-concealed looks of younger members of the human race observing your "pot" hanging over your belt. You try unobtrusively to slip into your Charles Atlas stance (only those who have reached middle age will remember him), but it's hopeless. Yet you continue on your way, hoping not too many people noticed your momentary digression.

On any given day at the beach, you will notice other middle-aged men with abdomens distended as if they were in the eighth month of pregnancy. Rather than being disturbed over their protrusions from their bodies, they *seem* to happily display their paunches almost as if they were trophies from a successful hunt. To make matters even worse, they adorn themselves with tight-fitting T-shirts that only accentuate their physique. They also demonstrate a disturbing tendency to pat their stomach as if it were some kind of a pet panda bear.

The Bible makes it quite clear that our bodies are the temples of the Holy Spirit. Paul asks, "Do you not know that your body is a temple of the Holy Spirit within you, which you have from God?" He then answers his own question. "You are not your own; you were bought with a price. So glorify God in your body." 1 Corinthians 6:19, 20, RSV. Should a temple be saggy, soft, and flabby? Should we neglect that wonderful creation we call a body? How does the care of this temple affect the male midlife crisis?

It is interesting to note that middle-aged men usually react to their bodies and health concerns in one of two extremes— compulsive concern or absolute neglect. Sometimes, they actually switch from one extreme to another at different stages of the crisis. They may become overcautious, hoping to stay young by keeping their bodies fit. In this case they usually go on extreme diets, lie under sun lamps (so as at least to look healthier), start jogging and exercising, and intermittently give up bad habits such as smoking and drinking. While the benefits of this regime are positive, they quickly discover that growing young is impossible—even if for a time they are able to compete with younger men on the racketball court. At the opposite extreme are the men who laugh at diet and exercise, drink and smoke as much as (or more than) ever, who shorten their life span by several years. As one wit put it, "The only exercise some people get these days is jumping to conclusions, running down their friends, sidestepping responsibilities, and pushing their luck"—especially the latter.

Given these two extremes, which one would you guess is the more likely to die of a heart attack? The easygoing fun-loving slob who eats too much, loves fatty foods, smokes two packs of cigarettes a day, never exercises, and has high blood pressure? Or, the impatient, competitive, type A behavior man who eats nothing but fresh fruits, salads, and non-fatty foods, wouldn't think of smoking, jogs three miles every day and has normal blood pressure? The answer—*both of them!*

Contrary to popular belief, Dr. Ray Rosenman, a pioneer in behavioral medicine, states that in some instances the "fun-loving slob" may actually outlive his type A counterpart. His research at Stanford University indicated that type A behavior midlife males were "two to three times more likely to have clogged coronary arteries or suffer heart attacks."[1] While recent evidence indicates that type A behavior is inherited as often as acquired, it is easily recognizable in the person who is extremely ambitious, aggressive, competitive, and impatient. He can be recognized almost anywhere by his irritability, tensed muscles, rapid movements, and emphatic speech. He is always rushing here and there, trying to accomplish the impossible. As a result, Dr. Rosenman concludes, "The type A person's adrenal glands secrete large quantities of a hormone called norepinephrine during most of the day. Too much of the hormone damages arteries and heart tissues."[2]

Apparently, how well you handle stress may more accurately determine your risk of heart attack than your diet. That is not to imply that an unhealthful diet is good for you or your heart! Quite the contrary! But stress is a major factor in heart attacks—besides being a major result of the midlife crisis. Dr. Rosenman's research reveals that middle-age American males have three times the rate of heart disease that French males do, even though Frenchmen eat more saturated fats, have higher blood pressures and higher levels of cholesterol in their blood. The big difference is one of behavior. It seems that the American male has eaten and is out of the restaurant and on his way to another project by the time the French male is through looking at the menu.

It is important to understand not only the stress of midlife, but what stress actually does to the body. The stress caused by emotional crises affects all the major physiological systems of the body. When the crisis is quickly resolved, the body suffers little ill effect. But when emotional stress becomes chronic, as it often does during midlife, the whole body may become so disrupted that the immune system breaks down, infections run rampant, and cell division gets out of control.

Our bodies are fearfully and wonderfully made. They have marvelous restorative powers. But they have their limitations. So what is the midlife male to do? His body is beginning to show visible signs of disrepair. Like an old building, the roof is in trouble, mortar is coming out of the joints, the floors are sagging, and the doors are beginning to creak. His problem: What do I do?

Fortunately, God has built into our bodies "early-warning" signs which, if heeded, help prevent their misuse. One of these early warning signs is fatigue. The causes of modern-day fatigue are varied, but only rarely the result of excessive physical exertion. The relatively few people who do heavy physical labor all day long seldom complain about being tired or fatigued. On the other hand, tiredness in today's society is usually the result of underexertion or lack of physical exercise. Increasing physical activity often eliminates that tired, run-down feeling known as fatigue.

With these facts in mind, it would be well for the midlife male to consider the three basic causes of fatigue as he examines his lifestyle.[3]

1. Physical: This is the result of overworking your muscles to the point where metabolic waste products (carbon dioxide and lactic acid) accumulate in your blood and sap your strength. Your muscles can't continue to work efficiently. Physical fatigue usually is a pleasant tiredness, such as you might experience after playing a hard set of tennis. The cure is simple and fast—you rest, giving your body a chance to get rid of accumulated wastes and restore muscle fuel.

2. Pathological: Here fatigue is a warning sign of the consequence of some underlying physical disorder, perhaps the common cold, flu, or something more serious like diabetes or cancer. Usually, other symptoms besides fatigue are present that suggest the true cause. Even after an illness has passed, you're likely to feel "dragged out" for a few weeks.

3. Psychological: Prolonged emotional problems and conflicts, especially depression and anxiety, are by far the most common causes of fatigue. Fatigue may be a defense mechanism that prevents you from having to face the true cause of your depression, such as the fact that you hate your job. It also is your body's safety valve for expressing repressed emotional conflicts, such as feeling trapped in an unrewarding role or an unhappy marriage.

During the male midlife crisis it is especially important to listen to your body's danger signals, especially fatigue. While going through this transition it would be a good time to reaffirm or perhaps establish some lifelong health habits that will make the remainder of your life more enjoyable and midlife crisis bearable.

1. Never smoke (if you currently are smoking **stop**).
2. Engage in physical activity on a regular basis.
3. Do not use unprescribed drugs or drink alcoholic or caffeinated beverages.
4. Get seven to eight hours sleep each night.
5. Maintain correct body weight for your height and skeletal structure. (Check your mirror if in doubt. It never lies.)
6. Eat a good breakfast. If you feel you must skip a meal, skip the evening meal.
7. Refrain from eating between meals.

The forty-five-year-old male who follows none to three of these health habits can expect to live another 21.6 years—or six months past his sixty-sixth birthday. However, the same man following six or seven of these health principles can expect to live another 33.1 years—or long enough to celebrate his seventy-eighth birthday. The choice is up to you, and the difference (for those not mathematically inclined) is 11.5 years.[4]

While it is true that we cannot change our inherited temperaments or perhaps even the stress of living in a competitive society, we can change ourselves to make the most of what we have. It is medically proven that those who exercise regularly (walking is a good exercise) can face middle age with greater equanimity; they are less tense, more secure, and suffer less depression than those who neglect exercising.

In addition to proper diet and sufficient exercise (at least three times a week), it is important for the midlife male to maintain (or cultivate) a sense of humor. The Bible reminds us, "A cheerful heart is a good medicine." Proverbs 17:22, RSV. "A glad heart makes a cheerful countenance. . . . A cheerful heart has a continual feast." Proverbs 15:13-15, RSV. "Anxiety in a man's heart weighs him down, but a good word makes him glad." Proverbs 12:25, RSV.

The most beneficial aspect of a good sense of humor is the tension release it provides. It is said that a hearty laugh can have the same tension-releasing value as a jog around the block or two Valium tablets. A good sense of humor enables us to laugh at ourselves during the midlife crisis, and can even help us cope with painful situations.

A quipper once remarked, "He who laughs last, laughs loudest." Perhaps we need to modify his advice, and simply say, "He who laughs—*lasts!*" Laughter is internal jogging. It is a message that goes from the inside out.

The late film star Edward G. Robinson offered some good advice: "If one takes himself seriously at all, he should smile; and if he starts taking himself even more seriously, he should laugh out loud." Cultivating a good sense of humor should receive a high priority on your midlife exercise list.

The following story appeared in the *Cincinnati Enquirer* (September 27, 1981) and illustrates what should be present in a well-rounded midlife exercise program.

The patient was a man in middle life who constantly complained of feeling ill. The doctor said to the man, "Charlie, I will give you a course of treatment that can cure you of what ails you and get you once again in vigorous good health. But do you really want to get well?"

"Of course, I want to get well," Charlie replied in injured tone. "Why do you think I keep coming to you?"

"First, every day I want you to take a three-mile walk.

Every single day, rain, shine, sleet or snow three miles each day, no less. That will take pressure off your brain, the pressure that comes from thinking and rehashing unhealthy thoughts of worry, tension and anxiety."

"But I play golf," Charlie said. "Do you want me to walk three miles even on a day when I play 18 holes of golf?"

"Absolutely. Golf is play. That's not the idea at all. Your three-mile walk is not to be play. It's to be something you do every single day as a vigorous self-discipline. And as you walk give thanks to God for everything you can think of: things like the sun, the rain, the snow; for giving you two good feet to walk with; for people you pass along the way; for your home; for your country; for every blessing you can possibly think of."

The doctor continued, "Second, make a list of persons who are worse off than you are, those who are in trouble or sorrow and go to them and do something for them."

Charlie looked blank. "Why," he said, "I wouldn't know what to say to them."

"Then go and say nothing. Just show your interest and friendliness. Let them see your good will. You'll find other ways to be helpful. If you don't know of anybody who's in trouble," he added, "I can sure give you names of plenty. And the third part of this program," he said, "is to read and reread the Gospel according to St. Luke. Over a period of time, see how much of it you can actually commit to memory." After outlining this strange prescription, he told his patient to come back and see him in two weeks.

You should see the man today. His heart action is the best it has ever been; blood pressure absolutely normal; his whole body vital, full of energy. He has new enthusiasm. Life to him is a lot better, and he takes pleasure doing things for people in trouble. He really enjoys trying to help them. And he quotes St. Luke by the paragraph. This man has actually had a renewal of the life force.

One of the most devastating symptoms of the male midlife is the tendency toward self-centeredness. We can quickly destroy our feeling of well-being by our unhealthy thinking and self-centered criticism of ourselves. By looking outside your own misery, you provide the most effective antidote known for depression and fatigue. Since most of the physical problems associated with male midlife crisis are the result of negative emotions, I would like you to review the following twelve principles outlined by psychologist Henry Knight Miller. Their proper use can help you gain freedom from those deadly destroyers known as depression, self-pity, self-depreciation, inferiority, and a whole host of other negative emotions:[5]

1. Think health, talk health, act health; and you will go a long way toward being healthy.
2. Be an actor, acting love instead of hate. What you act tends to become fact.
3. Shift your attention deliberately from the thing you are worrying about.
4. Cultivate opposites. If fearful, cultivate courage. If weak, cultivate strength. If gloomy, cultivate joy. Act as if you intend to become the opposite of what you are.
5. Rationalize your worries, hates, jealousies. Put them on the dissecting table; ruthlessly take them apart. You'll find there is very little substance to them.
6. Get a sense of the perspective of time and distance. How little our great worries seem, how unimportant our resentments, in the years after.
7. Cultivate optimism. Always look on the bright side. Keep the mouth lines up. Smile and be happy. William James claimed that we are happy because we smile rather than we smile because we are happy. In other words, the smile comes first.
8. Don't talk trouble. It only activates more of it. Talk life up, not down. Talking tends to create, for it puts the immense power of thought to work. Don't practice negative autosuggestion by the use of destructive words.
9. Develop other-centered vs. self-centered inter-

ests. Forget yourself in the great exciting world. One of the greatest of all laws is that he who forgets himself really finds himself.

10. Superimpose the positive on the negative. When a negative thought comes, practice canceling it with a positive thought and affirmation. Enough of this, and you will become positive in your attitudes.

11. Practice great affirmations like: "Life is good." "I believe." "People are wonderful." "God loves me." Such affirmations can lift you into the area of infinite powers.

12. Assert and dwell on your divine origin. Say to yourself every day, especially when things get dark and trouble stares you in the face, "I'm a child of God."

References

1. Tim DeBrosse, "Heart-Attack Victim Stereotype? He Doesn't Buy It," *St. Petersburg Times,* December 8, 1981.

2. *Ibid.*

3. "Modern-Day Fatigue," *Chicago Tribune,* February 19, 1980.

4. "You Too Can Live Longer," *Science News,* August 23, 1980, p. 117.

5. Norman Vincent Peale, "12 Principles Can Help Top Depression," *Cincinnati Enquirer,* October 11, 1981.

Work! A Dead-End Street?

There are many dead-end streets that lead to entrapment when a male is trying to deal with the midlife crisis. When you begin to feel sorry for yourself, you may be tempted to try any number of streets all of which have the same dead end. Some individuals turn to drugs or alcohol. Others decide to opt out of the rat race and retire early (but isn't forty-two a little too early?) Still others attempt to remake their bodies into late-twenties specifications. (Not that health isn't important; we have already covered the need of exercise in a previous chapter.)

I'll never forget the mental agony I went through trying to decide what to do with my bald head. When I first considered the possibility of getting a hairpiece (I was bald at twenty-four), I had to ask myself, "Why do you want a hairpiece? Is it going to help you relieve some youthful fantasy? What about vanity and all the words Solomon has to say concerning *that* dread malady? (Read the book of Ecclesiastes).

I wrestled with this problem for some time until one of my closest friends told me, "I really don't see your problem, Len, you are thirty years old and look fifty. You shouldn't be trying to look twenty again—only thirty." He was right. At thirty I looked fifty-five, because the only head hair I had was a "monk's ring." My friend gave me sound advice and the encouragement I needed some—and I have never regretted my decision. It made me feel better about myself. I became thoroughly convinced that God created the human head to be covered with hair. If anyone set out to eliminate hair, it could only have been Satan, and I was determined not to do any advertising for him.

Now, my hairpiece did not make me younger, physically, of course. But it did allow me to look my age. Nothing wrong with that, is there? On the other hand, we can expect too much from a hairpiece, a tanning-booth-tan, adult orthodontics, or rhinoplasty (nose surgery). While these may help our self-confidence (and that is vitally important) and improve our appearance, they will not work miracles and restore our lost youth. Sometimes unrealistic expectations along this line can actually lead to further and even more severe depression, when the reality of our age finally sinks in. All these attempts to regain our self-esteem through artificial means are temporary solutions at best.

However, there is one seemingly dead-end street that is socially acceptable and yet may be ultimately fatal—work! For most midlife males, work reveals vital information about who and what they are. It tells the world something about their self-worth. The worker who is approaching forty and has been making steady progress up the promotional ladder for almost two decades may suddenly find himself on a plateau with no further prospect of advancement. How is he to handle such a blow to his psyche and bank account? Especially when this condition occurs during a midlife crisis, brought on by other factors as well. Shall he give up the security he has earned over the past twenty years and take a chance with another company? Or, shall he whittle down his ambitions and goals to fit his circumstances?

At this juncture in a man's career his work becomes a two-edged sword with a sharp point. One "edge" tells him to buckle down and really work because the horde of youngsters a decade younger than he are nipping at his heels. The other "edge" says he has gone as far as he can in his career, so he must make a change. The "point" frequently is a heart attack caused by stress, overwork, and indecision. Here the man has spent twenty years getting halfway up the ladder, and now people half his age have more knowledge about the company when they graduate from college (thanks to computers), than he has after all his years of experience. Then one day he finds the corporation has changed his job description from "achiever" to "trainer." He is no longer climbing the corporate ladder of success but has been permanently assigned to one floor for the rest of his life. There is only room for "achievers" on the ladder. His achieving days are over. Our society, in which vocational achievement is seen as the most important indicator of male success, is an ideal environment for the condition known as the male midlife crisis.

Sören Kierkegaard, the Danish existentialist philosopher, once said, "When a man aspires to be a Caesar and fails to become a Caesar, he will hate what he is because he is not Caesar." One midlife male I know about, trapped in an occupation he didn't really like, complained, "Sure, I feel trapped. Why shouldn't I? Twenty-five years ago a dopey eighteen-year-old college kid made up *his* mind that *I* was going to be a dentist. So now here I am, a dentist. I'm stuck. What I want to know is, who told that kid he could decide what I was going to have to do for the rest of my life."[1]

The midlife male often feels impaled on the horns of a dilemma of his own devising. His obvious choices are either stay put, writhing in agony, in an occupation he dislikes, or push himself free and fall into the bottomless pit of nothingness known as unemployment and failure.

Many a wife fails to fully understand the intense terror her husband feels regarding his work. He has always come across as strong and secure. He has always seemed to know where he was going. To him, his job is an important part of his self-image and is interwoven into the very fabric of his being. The stress produced by unhappiness with his work combined with the fear of losing his job (and consequently his self-worth) produces unbelievable extremes in his emotional life as well as maladies such as ulcers, high blood pressure, colitis, impotence, and nervous breakdown.

If the midlife male chooses to change occupations or is fired from his job, what then? Upon what depths of reserves does he draw when his whole world is already topsy-turvy? A psychologist addressing the problem of "the care and feeding of the jobless man" stressed several important points for the wife to remember: "She should put the family on a very tight budget, make sure her husband's clothes are taken care of for job interviews, give him encouragement and special attention, take some care in what she says concerning family problems, refrain from nagging him to do household chores while he is at home and out of work, and keep up her own morale. With such a task before her the wife has as many pressures working on her as there are on her husband."[2]

I would further suggest the midlife male (whether "unhappily" employed or unemployed) enroll in a "success" course that will put him on the road to both positive and possibility thinking. His unemployment could actually be a blessing in disguise since he is free to try what he may have lacked the courage to attempt while still employed. It is also a time for him to become better acquainted with his own unique abilities through testing. Testing is available at most universities and technical schools. Remember that as you face the unknown, others have faced similar situations and have adjusted successfully.

George Foreman, one time heavyweight boxing champion of the world, found himself defeated at the peak of his career by Muhammad Ali. Picking himself up from the canvas, he gave himself to Christian service. He admits that he still misses boxing, but also contends that he has found more joy in bringing the gospel to lost souls than he ever did pounding someone to a pulp in the ring.

Albert Schweitzer, at the age of forty, had achieved international fame as one of the great interpreters of Bach. He had also written a book that became a theological classic among seminary students throughout the world. In addition, he was also a very wealthy man. Yet Schweitzer did not feel fulfilled, though he was obviously successful by the world's standards. At the age of forty he left it all behind and went to the interior of equatorial Africa to serve as a missionary to those who could never pay for his services.

Could there may be some latent talents or interest lying just beneath the surface of your midlife frustrations or insecurities? Oftentimes creative and imaginative people are never recognized by their contemporaries. Abraham Lincoln, for example, entered the Black Hawk War as a captain and came out a private. F. W. Woolworth got a job in a dry goods store when he was twenty-one, but his supervisors wouldn't let him wait on any customers because he "didn't have enough sense." Colonel Sanders of Kentucky-fried-chicken fame, became a millionaire, after most men would have retired, by promoting a chicken recipe he had been using in a little (going nowhere) roadside stand for years. The inventor of one of the most successful games ever created, Monopoly, was an unemployed worker in Atlantic City, New Jersey, during the Depression. He made up the game for his children because he couldn't afford to buy them any toys. As one man put it, "There is genius in the average man." We just need to know where to look and which button to push.

Those who fail in their quest for self-improvement often do so because they constantly think "sacrifice" rather than "possibility." By centering your attention upon achieving your goal, you make the obstacles seem smaller. By visualizing yourself as already attaining (and enjoying) your goal, you are more than halfway there. You need to turn your focus away from what you are giving up (i.e. security, income, etc.) and think instead about what you will gain. When your attention is focused upon the end result, to the exclusion of all else, the desire to do anything that might delay its fulfillment is lessened considerably. As the Greek philosopher Epictetus once said, "It is not the event, but one's viewpoint toward the event that is important."

Norman Vincent Peale, one of the most popular proponents of positive thinking, relates the following story concerning a midlife male's road to success: After stumbling along for years, one man suddenly found the secret of success.

This man changed remarkably in middle life and really began to go places and accomplish things. When I first knew him a few years ago, he was a likable guy who just wasn't getting anywhere. His personality was pleasant, but lacked force. The most engaging thing about him in those years was his ingratiating sociability. He never seemed to turn it off. Finally, I got suspicious this was partly a cover-up for some underlying sense of inferiority. That guess proved to be right.

As I got to know him better his frustrations came through and he admitted his failure as a person. He ever referred to himself disparagingly as a mediocrity. He just didn't seem to have what it takes, he would say glumly.

This admission gave me a first real glimpse of the painful inner self behind the supersociable exterior. It was that of a frustrated, deeply unhappy human being. We discussed his problem from time to time and I outlined a course of reading for him, including books that had triggered other people to more successful living.

Afterwards I asked this man how he explained his new success. I already knew the basic thing that had given him his new beginning: He had developed some sound spiritual faith which resulted in more faith in himself. But to go so far so fast, especially after his uninspired performance, he must have applied more positive faith consistently in specific ways and that was what I wanted to hear about.

In reply, he listed five rules by which he has learned to live more effectively. These are the secrets of his success.

First: "Be bold and mighty powers will come to your aid." That is a sentence from Basil King's book *The Conquest of Fear* and is a most significant statement. By fearfulness, by timidity, you cut yourself off from power—and I suspect this was one important factor in my friend's dilemma back before he found himself. But when you venture boldly, from the life force itself comes a flow of power potential. It is a law that dynamic powers emerge to the degree that you attack life boldly.

Second: Deny adverse conditions. Do not think, or say, "Conditions are against me" or "Things don't look good." Face facts, but realize it often happens that a person is defeated not by the facts of a situation, but by his negative interpretation of the facts. Avoid the subjective notion that conditions are adverse. Actually, they may only appear to be adverse. In every problem is an inherent good. Believe that every problem contains the seeds of its own solution.

Third: See and constantly picture good outcomes. By envisioning good, you actually bring good influences into play, both within yourself and in the world around you.

Fourth: Hold genuinely friendly thoughts for each client, customer or other business contact. See him benefitting from the dealings you have with him. Put him first in your thoughts. This will stimulate a reverse flow of values.

Fifth: Practice brotherly love toward everybody.[3]

When faced with the midlife trauma of employment (or lack of employment), it is time to take stock of who you are and where you want to be five or ten years from now. It doesn't matter so much where you have been or what successes have slipped from your grasp. The rest of your life begins **now**, this very moment. Determine to live each moment to the fullest. Determine to set your eyes upon worthwhile goals which include much more than money, houses, and things. The truly successful midlife male is one who has come to terms with the important issues of life.

Jesus summed up the real secret of midlife success (and self-worth) in this brief paragraph:

"This is my commandment, that you love one another as I have loved you. Greater love has no man than this, that a man lay down his life for his friends. . . . I chose you and appointed you that you should go and bear fruit and that your fruit should abide; so that whatever you ask the Father in my name, he may give it to you. This I command you, to love one another." John 15:12-17, RSV.

It is genuine love for his fellow man that will bring lasting self-esteem to the midlife male. This concept, advocated by Jesus for success in all of your life, is further defined by Paul in his letter to the Christians living in Corinth. "Love is patient and kind; love is not jealous or boastful; it is not arrogant or rude. Love does not insist on its own way; it is not irritable or resentful; it does not rejoice at wrong, but rejoices in the right. Love bears all things, believes all things, hopes all things, endures all things." 1 Corinthians 13:4-7, RSV.

When you work to establish love in your life, you will find both immediate and eternal rewards. Such work will never be a dead-end street. You will find that you truly succeed when those with whom you come in contact are also successful. The dog-eat-dog concept frequently precipitates the midlife crisis. The love principle turns all things (including midlife) into eternal success.

References

1. Barbara Fried, *The Middle-Age Crisis* (New York: Harper & Row, 1967), p. 59.

2. Lee, p. 150.

3. Norman Vincent Peale, "Here Are Five Simple Rules to Success," *Cincinnati Enquirer,* November 29, 1981.

Is There Sex After Midlife?

"The most pernicious of all sexual fictions is the nearly universally accepted belief that sexual effectiveness inevitably disappears as the human being ages. It simply isn't true."—William H. Masters and Virginia E. Johnson.

Even with that carefully researched and fully documented statement by two of the most prominent researchers in the area of sexual function and dysfunction, many midlife males not only fear impotency, but actually experience it. In his article "On Taking Sex Seriously," Tom Driver reminds us that "laughter at sex is about the only way to put sex in its place. . . . And he who does not laugh about it must be humiliated by it."[1] However, failure to achieve an erection is far from being a laughing matter for most midlife males.

A prominent urologist has been quoted as saying, "What happens above a man's neck is vastly more important than what happens below his belt." While researchers agree that there is no physical reason why a healthy man cannot continue to have sexual intercourse well into his eighties, poor sexual performance by midlife males is quite common. However, the vast majority of causes are psychological and not physical. Achieving an erection is largely a psychological process which can be hindered by a variety of tensions or anxieties. Generally speaking, a male finds his self-worth in two areas of his life, his career and his sexual prowess. His ability to advance in his chosen career and his ability to both arouse and satisfy his wife are two major criteria in the life of the midlife male. However, dur-

59

ing midlife, a man's sexual capacity (or lack of it) may become his single greatest concern. He may be afraid he is losing his sexual appeal as well as his sexual ability. The drama goes something like this: A man is overextended at work, trying to ward off the "young bucks" seeking to take his position. He is running out of energy. He is on innumerable boards and committees for both his community and church. His family makes great financial demands, with the children in college or late high school, and there never seems to be enough money to pay all the bills. Surrounded by all these pressures, is it any wonder he simply crawls in between the sheets and tries to go to sleep?

At the same time his wife is probably experiencing a new sexual awakening. Instead of being the passive "little woman" she has become more aggressive in her approaches. To his chagrin, he discovers he is extremely slow in rising to the occasion, and worse yet, halfway through their lovemaking he unexplainably wilts. Suddenly he concludes that life is over for him. He is no longer a man. He's a failure.

As he rolls over and tries to go to sleep, he wonders what is causing the problem. Is it his wife's new zest for sex that threatens his manhood, or is his wife losing her ability to arouse him? For a fleeting moment he sees a glimmer of hope. Maybe it isn't him after all. Perhaps a change of sex partners would solve his problem.

Any man tempted to choose this option should remember that it's hard to live it down when you've been living it up. The real test of married love is remaining faithful to one's spouse in spite of physiological changes. A husband and wife who still arouse each other sexually after thirty or forty years can be much more proficient in the art of making love than the celebrities who infest the gossip columns with a different partner every month. The sexual athlete who bounces from pillow to bedpost usually winds up sleeping with other rejects like himself.

But how does the panic-stricken midlife male put the zip back in his sex life without changing sexual partners? It must be remembered that most of us become creatures of habit, and getting into a rut is a good way to kill one's sex life. From a purely practical viewpoint, the end of the evening—commonly referred to as "bedtime"—is the least favorable time for sex during midlife, for the simple reason that physical energy is usually at its lowest ebb at that time. In addition, the accumulated mental pressures of the day tend to make it the least ideal time to rejuvenate the libido. One writer contends that one of the most revealing aspects of extramarital midlife affairs is that the lovemaking takes place at odd hours during the day. If this be true, why not try to find opportunities at other times of day when sex with one's spouse better coincides with the peaks of one's physical and emotional levels. Making love in the morning or at lunchtime can bring back lost passion and put some real zest into your marital relationship. Why do you think the Europeans have such long lunch breaks?

Another secret to sexual rejuvenation in midlife is to do the unexpected. Be open to change and experimentation. God created men and women to enjoy sex. If you will think back, bringing together the sex partners was God's crowning act for His created inhabitants of earth that first Friday afternoon. Their marriage by God was intended to complete their "one flesh" experience. "One flesh" means a complete union physically, emotionally, and spiritually. Sex provides the opportunity for two distinct individuals to lose themselves in each other and, in the process, experience some of the most exquisite feelings possible for two human beings.

Get out of your sexual "rut" and find new ways to enjoy this most intimate of all relationships. It is not surprising that the leading cause of male impotence is monotony in the sex act. Note the reasons given by the Masters and Johnson research team given in order of importance:[2]

1. Monotony of repetitious relationship.
2. Preoccupation with career or economic pursuits.
3. Mental or physical fatigue.
4. Overindulgence in food or drink.
5. Physical and mental infirmities of a man or his spouse.
6. Fear of failure in the sex act.

Preoccupation with career or economic pursuits was illustrated quite clearly as a cause of impotence when the bottom dropped out of the stock market in 1929. Men who were worth fortunes on paper were literally wiped out financially and left penniless overnight—in some cases in a single hour. While we will never know how many were made temporarily impotent by the crash, it was routine to hear women say that they had not had sexual relations with their husbands for six months after Black Thursday, when the stock market collapsed.[3]

Where does the midlife male turn to remedy his impotency? Few go to their family physicians (it is too embarrassing), and even fewer go to a psychiatrist or psychologist (it is their wife's problem, not theirs). Unfortunately, the common recourse for "curing" impotency is another woman. Because the midlife man is successful in having sex with a new sex partner, he concludes erroneously that the fault lies with his wife. What he fails to realize is that much of his newfound "success" is due to the fact that monotony has not yet set in to his new relationship. If and when his new sex partner becomes available to him every day (or night), he is likely to find his old impotency problem reacurring.

Our society tempts couples into affairs in many ways. The mass media advertises these episodes on afternoon and evening soap operas. We refer to them lightly as "having a fling" or "fooling around," which sounds much less condemnatory than *adultery*. In the first blush of new "love," affairs seem to be fun and ego-boosting. As Solomon puts it, "Stolen waters are sweet" (Proverbs 9:17), but in the end they usually turn bitter.

Why then do they taste sweet, at first? Your spouse may be taking you for granted, but your lover doesn't. One of the great "turn-ons" in an affair is the positive strokes the lovers give each other. She tells him what a man he is. He tells her she is sensuous. Many times, the midlife male is so enraptured by these "feelings" that have lain dormant since his honeymoon, that he leaves his wife and marries the one with whom he is having the affair.

How do affairs begin? Where do they begin? With whom do they begin? The answers are anything, anywhere, and anyone.

It can happen between family friends or neighbors, over a cup of hot chocolate at work, on an out-of-town trip, with a former flame not forgotten, with a lawyer, a doctor, or a counselor, and with a married woman who is simply out "scoring" to boost her own misguided ego.

It is a contradiction that we teach our children the accepted traditional code of marriage, yet, so often, we live a lie completely contrary to what we teach. Apparently, for some, teaching fidelity in marriage is almost like teaching children about Santa Claus; when they grow up they really don't expect their children to believe in it anymore. For a Christian, being caught in the trap of misguided sexual mores can be especially devastating. The guilt of adultery only compounds the emotional trauma already being experienced by the midlife male.

The Bible faithfully records the experiences of men, both good and bad. One such man was David, the shepherd boy who killed Goliath with his slingshot, the warrior king who reclaimed all the promised land for God's people. Here he stands at the pinnacle of power, having accomplished what few men have ever dared to dream—and he is *bored*! One dismal day, while strolling on the terrace of his royal garden he spotted a beautiful woman bathing in an adjoining courtyard. Two fatal ingredients for midlife male infidelity came together on that afternoon—she was young and beautiful, and he was bored. (See 2 Samuel 11 and 12.)

Once David took a "second" look, his life seemed to go out of control. Later, his conscience confirmed the wrongness of the affair. He tried to quiet it, but he couldn't. Failing in that, he tried to salve his conscience (Bathsheba was pregnant) by bringing her husband back from the battle front to spend a few days (and nights—presumably) with his wife, hoping perhaps that Uriah would think he made his wife pregnant. But Uriah refused to be fooled, even when David got him drunk.

In desperation, David took matters into his own hands. He sent Uriah back to the front bearing a message to Joab, his commander, instructing the latter to let Uriah be killed so that it would look "natural." In the battle that followed Uriah lost his life.

Now David had two problems on his guilt-ridden conscience—adultery and murder. After God confronted the king's perfidy through Nathan the prophet, and David repented of his great wrongs, he wrote the following psalm:

> Blessed is he whose transgression is forgiven,
>   whose sin is covered.
> Blessed is the man to whom the Lord imputes no iniquity,
>   and in whose spirit there is no deceit.
> When I declared not my sin, my body wasted away
>   through my groaning all day long.
> For day and night thy hand was heavy upon me;
>   my strength was dried up as by the heat of summer.
> I acknowledged my sin to thee,
>   and I did not hide my iniquity;
> I said, "I will confess my transgressions to the LORD";
>   then thou didst forgive the guilt of my sin.
> Therefore let every one who is godly
>   offer prayer to thee;
> at a time of distress, in the rush of great waters,
>   they shall not reach him.
> Thou art a hiding place for me,
>   thou preservest me from trouble;
>   thou dost encompass me with deliverance."
>   Psalm 32:1-7, RSV.

David's experience can help the midlife male who feels trapped in the prison of guilt. While David could not forgive himself, he realized that if he confessed and forsook his sin, God could and would forgive him. Reading and rereading David's song of sincere repentance may provide a model for others in their quest for forgiveness and elimination of the unbearable burden of guilt.

How does one go about cleaning up the mess created by an affair? The sooner one begins the better. But where do you begin? Before answering these questions let me remind all midlife males that your wife is an important part of any decision you now make about an affair you have had or are currently having. Because both the husband and wife have individual and quite different responses to an extramarital affair and any attempt to restore the marriage afterward, it is unfair to group them together in their roles of restoring the marriage.

The Husband: When the Holy Spirit convicts a man that he is living in sin, he should, immediately begin to build bridges back toward his wife, while at the same time he *must* burn *all* bridges he has built toward his lover. I have counseled some men who were willing to burn most of the bridges, but not that *final* bridge to their lover. They wanted to leave a "footbridge"—just in case. . . . There is no guarantee, of course, that a wife will take back an adulterous husband, but being unwilling to burn *all* the bridges undercuts the sincerity of a man's repentance and lessens his chances of a reconciliation with his wife.

A man must begin by being honest with himself. He must answer candidly the question, How did I get into this mess?

It is easy and perhaps convenient to answer that it was somebody else's fault—his wife, his lover, but not his. It is at this point that some midlife males begin to juggle the books of married life. The adulterer "intends" to talk things through with his spouse, to clear up all their "misunderstandings," to work out the differences between them, but when it comes right down to it, too often such "intentions," if carried out, simply turn into an opportunity for the guilty party to vent his hostility and anger at his spouse and to "confirm" the hopelessness of the situation. And the natural reaction is for his mate to respond with similar anger and hostility. Not being truly honest with himself or his wife, such a midlife male is doomed to failure at worst, and an armed truce at best.

One midlife male who came to me asked in a sincere moment of reflection: "What do I get out of this affair? Surely it is not what I got with my wife, not at all. So why do I do it? To make myself feel young again, I suppose—to get away with something—to prove I can still be attractive to younger women—maybe just to relieve the monotony of our marriage. I don't know. But, if my wife is so wonderful, why isn't she enough for me? I wish I knew. She loves me and I love her, and that is very nice, very comforting. But it leaves me feeling middle-aged and over-the-hill, and I'm not willing to accept this conclusion—at least not yet. I'm confused. I know I'll never find anyone like my wife again, yet I run after women I don't care about. I play the game, I chase them, I make love to them, and I go home feeling good—for a little while. But the truth is, I'm not happy. So, you figure that out!"

Another misguided midlife male lamented, "I'll never forget how my wife acted, when she learned about my cheap little affair with the girl at the office. I knew it must be hurting her terribly, but she didn't whine or complain, or even strike out at me. She sat me down, looked me straight in the eyes, and asked me where *she* had gone wrong. Where had *she* failed me? What did this girl have that *she* didn't? At that moment I knew what a fine person my wife really was, and I felt really ashamed of the whole sordid business. From that moment onward the other woman didn't have a chance."

As the tempted midlife male sorts out the "facts of life," he should compare his "new love" with the "original." Does his new partner really deliver a superior form of love? She may seem like a fresh and desirable "new beginning"—but beginning of what? Ideally he will realize that his "new beginning" is merely the delusive hope of rejuvenating his lost youth. If he looks in the mirror, he will realize that when his "new beginning" reaches his age, he will be retired, wrinkled, and gray. Will he then be proud he yielded to temptation?

The Wife: The first question that usually comes to the mind of a woman when she suspects her husband is having an affair is, What do I do now? The most important thing to remember is to do *nothing* immediately! Don't jump into action or to conclusions; instead, do a little reflecting. A woman should consider what this affair is saying about her, about her husband, about their relationship, and about their marriage. She should try to discover why her husband is having the affair, what the needs are in his life that are not being met, what attractions he sees in the other person, and what she should do to remedy the situation. Outbursts of passion and anger seldom, if ever, win friends and influence people. Although she may feel angry and betrayed, the wiser course is to approach the problem with patience and understanding. Gestapo methods do not work in these kinds of situations. The wife must decide whether she wants revenge or her marriage. There is no question but what she has been wronged, but the question is, Is her marriage worth saving? That must be her major concern during this difficult period.

Wives are often surprised to learn that an affair often doesn't happen because a man is looking for better sex. In many instances, a husband may be looking for kinds of attention he has not been finding at home. In such cases a wife may have to assure her husband that she really wants to meet his needs and is willing to learn how to accomplish that task—and then proceed to put her words into action! One couple I counseled told me that if they never got out of bed, their marriage would be terrific. They were perfectly matched as physical lovers, but horribly mismatched as marriage partners. Their marriage was in shambles, and neither one seemed willing to do what was necessary to put it back together.

If the marriage is to be mended, a wife must be able to forgive her wayward husband. She must decide up front whether or not she is willing to forgive and forget—even though she will never forget. Most Christians think they must forget if they are to really forgive, but when you think about it, if you could really forget there would be no need to forgive. The essential element is forgiveness. Forgiveness may not be easy, but it is indispensable if the marriage is to survive.

After the initial shock of learning about the affair wears off, the wife will usually experience a full range of emotions including anger, confusion, and self-pity. One of the most common emotions resulting from a husband's affair is intense emotional hurt: "How could he do this to me?" As the wife ponders her hurt, she begins to question every aspect of her own being. She will probably feel betrayed, rejected, cheated. Her self-image will plummet, perhaps close to zero.

The emotional stages through which a betrayed wife goes are usually denial, reluctant acceptance, anxiety, grief, anger, and finally a decision to continue or terminate the marriage. If the wife fails to complete this emotional process, her emotional upheaval tends to continue unabated and makes it extremely difficult for her to reach a decision. These various stages are similar to those her unfaithful husband is going through as he examines his life. Each stage must be adequately dealt with in order eventually to find emotional peace and contentment.

If a wife decides her marriage is worth preserving, she should be aware of the nature of her husband's male ego. As already pointed out, man's ego is especially vulnerable during the sex act. His inability to function can destroy his concept of himself as a man. The least hint by the wife that he is inadequate in his lovemaking can be devastating. A wise woman will therefore look for legitimate ways in which she can strengthen his self-image.

There are other things a wife can do. As one author put it, "A woman can show her love by being more alluring. With all the helps available for ladies today to improve themselves, there is no excuse for her to look like a leftover from a garage sale.... A twinkle in her eye and a smile on her face will tell him that she is happy to see him, and if he smells dinner cooking in the background, he will surely know it."[4]

A final reminder to both the midlife male and his wife concerning preventive maintenance for their marriage *before* an affair develops. One of the reasons for sex life slipping into the "dull"-drums is that it has become too predictable. We no longer court and care. We have become hurried and habitual. We no longer dress attractively or shower frequently for our mates. We no longer encourage each other's self-image. We fail to provide the atmosphere that says we care about and need our spouse.

References

1. Tom F. Driver, "On Taking Sex Seriously," *Christianity and Crisis,* October 14, 1963, p. 177.

2. Henry Still, *Surviving the Male Mid-Life Crisis* (New York: Thomas Y. Crowell, 1977), pp. 82, 83.

3. Stanley Frank, *The Sexually Active Man Past Forty* (New York: The MacMillan Company, 1968), p. 74.

4. Tim and Bev LaHaye, *Spirit-Controlled Family Living* (Old Tappan, N.J.: Fleming H. Revell Co., 1978), p. 95.

The Midlife Marriage

Jean Moreau once said, "Age doesn't protect you from love. But love, to some extent, protects you from age." Most of us have heard the old cliché, "They've been married so long they are beginning to look alike." In actual fact, couples don't grow to be alike during the course of a marriage, according to a recent study. While it is true that some assimilate their spouse's habits, there is no general trend that suggests couples become more similar physically with age. In fact, most research indicates the opposite to be true and offers some interesting insights regarding the midlife period, particularly with respect to divorce and remarriage.[1] Here are some of the findings:

Rather than making a marriage happier, children tend to produce the opposite effect, at least while they are growing up.

Communication and expression of love often decline with length of marriage.

The longer some couples are married, the less well they seem to know each other.

In compiling the results of such studies, it soon becomes apparent that the couples interviewed (who remained together in marriage) tended to fall into one of two general categories:

1. Golden Sunset. These couples say, "It gets better every year." Not that they haven't had problems in their marriage, but they never considered wanting to be married to someone else. A common thread running through these marriages is that they spend a lot of time together.

2. Survivors. These marriages are little more than an endurance contest or a test of willpower. It is not really a happy union, but they can proudly (if not happily) say, "We've made it!" In fact, that was the most common reply heard from the "survivors."

Obviously, since the foregoing study was only dealing with long-term marriages, it revealed little of the trauma associated with broken homes or divorced couples. However, the researchers did find that for most couples marital happiness begins to decline after the children are in school. The reverse is true when the children leave home. It would seem that the empty-nest syndrome, at least in long-term marriages, is more than compensated for by an increase in marital happiness and satisfaction. A general consensus of the couples interviewed was, "These are the best years of our marriage."

Unfortunately, many couples never stay together long enough to see that upward swing in their marriage relationship. The divorce rate seems to peak around the twentieth year of marriage and generally coincides with the male midlife crisis. Several important factors seem to converge upon the marriage at this crucial point in time:

1. The children are almost through (high) school or have already finished.
2. The demands of his (and her) career is at its peak.
3. Communication has declined over the years as the children and career demanded most of their time and energy.
4. The financial burden of continuing education for their children is a reality.
5. The husband is in his midlife years.

It is at this point that irritants and disagreements that have existed in the relationship for years now become almost unbearable. These irritants have been ignored, now they have festered into running sores. Because the midlife male often fails to understand the reasons for his restlessness and depression, he finds it increasingly more easy to blame his wife. He begins to feel that their marriage was a mistake from the beginning and has never brought more than fleeting happiness at best. He exaggerates the negatives in the marriage because he is looking through eyes filled with self-pity and depression.

Unfortunately, his wife is usually unprepared to accept this blame and rejection, because she doesn't understand what is happening to her husband. So, rather than responding with patience and understanding (which is difficult when living with a midlife male), she begins to prepare a complaint list of her own and acts in a defensive manner.

If the midlife couple could objectively review their complaint list, they would find that most of their problems are the result of marriage enemy number one, boredom! Familiarity breeds contempt, according to the popular saying. In marriage such familiarity is a prophecy of doom. We grow accustomed to what is in front of us every day until we no longer see it. The painting that hangs over the fireplace no longer evokes our admiration or even a quick glance. Likewise, the companion that sits across from us at the breakfast table is no longer electrifying, fascinating, absorbing.

For a while this situation may seem tolerable. We ignore what is obviously happening because we do not wish to create a problem by bringing it up. But, as the years go by and we realize that this boredom may be our lot in life until the grave, a sort of desperation begins to set in. There must be more to life than this we reason: Surely there must be at least one more opportunity to capture the intensity I felt as a newlywed.

Marriage must conquer the monster of habit, or it will surely devour the couple. Soon the marriage partners are no longer satisfied by the stimuli offered. Something else is needed. Habit, routine, sameness, emptiness, disenchantment, the feeling of being taken for granted, the "blah's," a lack of any real value, all tend to point toward an affair or a divorce. The deadly thing about marriage is not the conflict—but the habit ruts. Once these ruts are established, it becomes increasingly difficult to go in any other direction. And as one wit has remarked, "A rut is nothing more than a grave open at both ends."

For those who fall into the habit rut, sexual problems tend to intensify. When boredom sets in, desire is elbowed out. Arguments become more heated, and this only causes more problems. The wife can't understand why her husband always tries to "patch things up with sex," and the husband can't understand why his wife "feels used." If these problems are to be successfully resolved, the underlying misunderstandings must be discussed openly and empathetically. Each partner must put himself in the shoes of the other person and try to understand the position from which the other is speaking. This is vital to productive communication. The problem is that too often emotions become the significant factor in the midlife marriage, and communication is lost in the maelstrom of emotions.

In addition to the midlife male problems already discussed in previous chapters, the midlife marriage must often withstand the strain of a tense and fatigued wife. The constant tension in the marriage makes her tired. Sometimes her fatigue is so great she would willingly drop, but she feels she must keep going so things won't get any worse. In some cases waiting up for her husband or engaging in a late-night argument robs her of sleep. To further complicate matters, she may begin to overeat or not eat enough of the right foods. Ulcers, acne, menstrual complications, headaches, heart trouble and other symptoms may be the result of the stress her body is going through.

Some men physically abuse their wives during this time in their marriage. In his anger and frustration over unresolved issues in their relationship, a formerly gentle husband can become a violent and uncontrollable stranger. Needless to say, this can be the breaking point in their marriage. However, if they make it through this trauma, the chances are good that they will remain together for the rest of their lives.

At the present time, in any given year, there are approximately two million marriages and one million divorces in America. Divorce has become not only accepted, but also a way of life. Obviously, by the time most couples go to a marriage counselor, what they are really looking for is emotional support for an impending divorce, not some way to put their marriage back together. Since many of these divorces take place during the midlife period, it is important to understand why the husband leaves home and later allows (often uncontested) his wife to dissolve the marriage. In many cases, of course, she is the injured party because of an affair and has every right to dissolve the marriage. In other instances he may simply leave home in order to escape the tension of marriage. He wants time to be alone, to sort things out. Home only reminds him of his obligations and the needs of his spouse. But these are not the only reasons midlife males leave home.

Some men leave home because they think it will be best for the family. They may actually think they are losing their minds and that their family would be better off without them. Unable to cope with their vacillating moods and temper tantrums, they decide to leave before they do something they may regret. Other midlife males are actually driven out of the home by the wife or family. No one seems to understand what is happening to the husband and father. Unable or unwilling to cope with this stranger in their home, they cast him out at the time of his greatest need of support.

In their counseling of midlife males, Jim and Sally Conway report, "Men have told us their wives have laughed at them or chided them for breaking down and crying over their confusion about who they were, work problems, or any of the many other things men wrestle with in mid-life. . . . Many men have seen little alternative but to leave."[2]

On the other hand, some men leave simply because they are tired of the "original" and want to trade her in for a "later model." One midlife male exclaimed, "I want happiness, love, approval, admiration, sex, youth. All this is denied me in this stale marriage to an elderly, sickly, complaining, nagging wife. Let's get rid of her, start life over again with another woman. Sure, I'll provide for my first wife and my children; sure, I'm sorry that the first marriage didn't work out. But self-defense comes first; I just *have* to save myself."[3]

With all of these and many other reasons causing separations in the midlife marriage is there really any hope of a couple staying together once the fester has begun? The answer is an emphatic Yes! But it requires work, *work*—and more **work!** Three of the most common aspects of any relationship are

(1) Communication, (2) Sharing, and (3) Self identity and self-understanding. If the midlife couple is fully aware of their own thoughts, feelings, and intentions, as well as the wants, needs, and desires of their mates, they have taken a giant step toward building a better marriage.

Assuming that both partners agree there is a problem in their marriage, what steps should they take to smooth over and heal the situation? Sometimes the biggest problem is not knowing what the problem really is. Couples may wrestle with trying to identify the problem for some time before it finally emerges. Couples don't like to admit they might have made a mistake, so often they deny there is a problem. Denial is the one factor that keeps many unhappy, unsatisfying marriages together. It also prevents them from seeking help. Other than divorce, what exactly are some alternatives for the midlife marriage crisis?

My first suggestion is that you begin to build a library of self-help books dealing with the midlife crisis, communication, listening, and other aspects of your current situation. In addition, there are many enrichment courses and seminars being offered by schools and churches in almost every community which will help any willing couple find their own identity, as well as identify their problems. One nationwide network I highly recommend is Marriage Encounter, sponsored by the Catholic, Lutheran, and Seventh-day Adventist churches throughout North America. Other seminars will help you develop communication skills, proper family "fighting"(discussion) skills, and how to listen intelligently. Whatever you spend on seminars or self-help materials will be returned to you a hundredfold by the change that can take place in you and your marriage.

In addition to these sources of help, couples need to take off their rose-colored glasses and begin to look at life, marriage, and the pursuit of happiness from a realistic viewpoint. They need to talk to each other openly and honestly about their expectations of themselves, their relationship to each other, and their marriage. The romantic view that love will take care of everything is unrealistic and true only if you know where to apply the healing balm of selfless love. Couples must learn to communicate and share; otherwise emotional distance inevitably comes between them and causes more problems.

At the risk of being too simplistic, here are a few basic guidelines for the couple seeking to increase their communication skills:

1. Speak for yourself, and let your partner do the same.

2. Stop and listen to what you are saying. Are you using phrases such as "If you only loved me, then you would . . . ?"

3. Recognize that your partner may have a hard time saying what she (he) wants to say and thus assumes you understand and agree with her (him). Learn to repeat what your partner has just said, in your own words, and see if you really understand what was said.

4. Recognize that your partner is not a mind reader. Say directly what you are feeling.

5. Take responsibility for your own feelings and thoughts. To do so will mean taking a risk, but it is worth it. Your partner may be waiting for you to quit blaming and start assuming the responsibility.

6. Be prepared to be hurt and frustrated at times. Recognize that "this too shall pass." Loving means taking a chance to let your partner grow, and in the process you too will grow and mature in your relationship.

But what can the wife do, if after all this her husband still leaves home? The first thing she can do is close her mouth! *Literally!* It is better if the news of her husband's leaving doesn't travel to too many people immediately. He may only be gone a few days and want to return. The wife can make it almost impossible for him to return if she has told all their mutual friends that he has left. One of the basic "reentry" problems for the midlife male is loss of face. When he left he "burned all his bridges behind him." Now, after thinking it over, he would like to rebuild those bridges. He may have cut himself off from neighbors, friends, church family, and others when he left his immediate family.

At this point, the wife can be helpful, or she can make it almost impossible for him to return. If she feels that he ought to make public apologies or come crawling home on his hands and knees, begging forgiveness, then she is in for a disappointment. His pride will see to that. On the other hand, if she uses her head, and her husband does decide to return home, if she has told no one, so much the better.

Another "reentry" problem is the husband's need to cut off the relationships he has developed while being away from home. In the "single" world he has probably established relationships that will not wear well once he returns to married life. Here again he faces the problem of losing face. What he needs to remember is that reentry will never work if he tries to keep one foot in each door of two lives.

In the male midlife crisis, reentry is never easy—*but it is possible!* Basically, the success or failure of reentry falls more heavily upon the wife than the husband. While it is true that she was the injured party and he probably deserves to be punished, if she hopes to reestablish the marriage on a secure basis, she will forgo the pleasure of punishing him. This may seem unfair, and it is, but then which is more important, the marriage or revenge?

A wife needs to bear in mind that at this point her errant spouse may not fully appreciate the pain he has caused his spouse, but reminding him of this will only create further friction and alienation. At the moment of reentry he neither needs a hovering mother or nagging shrew. What he needs and wants is an understanding girlfriend. If his wife becomes his girlfriend, she satisfies this need.

For the truly discerning midlife wife, attempting to put her marriage back together, Josephine Lowman offers the following tips on the likes and dislikes of the average male.[4]

Men like:

1. A sense of humor. This adds fun to everyday life.
2. Kindness and gentleness.
3. Makeup, if they don't know you have it on, or at least if it is natural enough to look real. They even enjoy a bit of dramatization on special occasions.
4. A good figure, but curves, not thinness.
5. They are drawn to vitality and aliveness, but not to the woman who is the "life" of the party.

6. They appreciate tact in a woman.
7. Most of all they like a woman who makes life seem easy and uncomplicated.
8. Naturalness.

Men do not like:
1. Cattiness, snide remarks about other women.
2. They do not like new styles at first, but usually like them after they become accustomed to them.
3. They hate complaining, but enjoy household chatter if it is humorous or interesting.
4. They do not like the siren type. She makes them feel uneasy.
5. They do not like to hear about your former conquests or boyfriends.
6. They have a horror of becoming involved in long emotional discussions.
7. Generally, they do not like candlelight at the dinner table (this author must be an exception because I love it!) but succumb to it with enthusiasm, if the mood of festivity or relaxation and good conversation go along with it. Otherwise, they want to see their food clearly so they can concentrate on it.
8. Fretting drives them crazy.

Psychologists tell us we tend to forget unpleasant experiences while remembering those that were pleasing or shared. In other words, we remember the "good ole days" and forget the bad memories to a great degree. Therefore, it is important in every marriage that the partners share enough pleasant experiences so they can look back on the "good old days." Marriages become boring when there is a lack of shared experiences. Each time you and your spouse have fun together you are, in effect, making a deposit in your savings account. Your marriage can draw a lot of accumulated interest over the years and may provide enough withdrawals during the midlife to sustain the marriage.

It is also important that each marriage partner be encouraged to develop his or her own interests and potential. If this is pursued on an individual basis, part of the shared pursuit may be to encourage your partner in his or her individual development. Whether it is music or mechanics, gardening or art, sewing or restoring antiques, encouraging your partner in his area of interest and expertise will help bridge the midlife marriage gap through mutual sharing.

Sally Conway in her book *You and Your Husband's Mid-Life Crisis* offers the following advice to the midlife wife: "A key to mid-life marriage restoration is your willingness to recognize that you are a part of the existing dissatisfaction. True, he is the other part. But your responsibility lies with *your* contribution to the marriage relationship. You need to confess your failures, stubbornnesses, insensitivities, and other faults that have undermined the happiness of your marriage. You need to tell God you are sorry and tell your husband you are sorry."[5]

References

1. Joan Sweeney, "Longevity Affecting Marriage as Much as Social Climate," *Indianapolis Star,* June 24, 1982.

2. Sally Conway, p. 79.

3. Edmund Bergler, *The Revolt of the Middle-Aged Man* (New York: Grosset and Dunlap, 1954), pp. 75, 76.

4. Josephine Lowman, "Why Grow Old?" *The Champaign-Urbana* (Illinois) *News-Gazette,* January 24, 1980.

5. Sally Conway, p. 187.

Help!

When Solomon wrote the book of Ecclesiastes he had developed a very pessimistic attitude. In his passion for observation he had insisted on seeing "everything under the sun." As a result of his research and analysis, he came to the conclusion that "all is vanity and a striving after wind." Ecclesiastes 1:14, RSV. For some, his experience may be a welcome antidote to the superficial optimism often found in self-help, positive-type books on the market today. Certainly the "preacher's" realistic look at life in his declining years offers an honest (if not hopeful) look at life's problems.

Most of us prefer not to look at life as honestly as the author of Ecclesiastes. We have a way of convincing ourselves that if we ignore the problem long enough it will go away. We tend to look at the "silver lining" and give no thought to the darkness surrounding the actual problem itself. Thomas Hardy put it appropriately when he commented, "If a way to the better there be, it exacts a full look at the worst."

Midlife must be faced with what may be called "provisional pessimism" before it can result in "ultimate optimism." By this I mean, we need to accept the fact that the trouble and pain are real, before we can finally emerge with hope. We need to realistically appraise the situation before we find our way to any sort of intelligent confidence. Of course, we should not live in anticipation of trouble, disappointment, and pain. On the contrary, it is wise to live on the assumption that when trouble comes, we can meet it with creative courage and the hope of success. As

81

Robert Browning noted, "Trouble is just the stuff to try the soul's strength, educe [to draw out] the man."

David Harum's advice is more homespun but much easier to understand: "A few fleas is good for a dog. They keep him from thinking about being a dog." While the midlife male may not appreciate the "fleas" that have suddenly come into his life, he can certainly appreciate the fact that those "fleas" now have his complete attention. He will feel much better when the "fleas" leave, and he will forever after be able to empathize with another dog with fleas.

Yet, we can have confidence as we approach any problem in life with the strength of Jesus in our corner. The Bible reassures us that, "No temptation [problem] has overtaken you that is not common to man. God is faithful, and he will not let you be tempted [tested] beyond your strength, but with the temptation [problem] will also provide the way of escape, that you may be able to endure it." 1 Corinthians 10:13, RSV. This promise also applies to the male midlife crisis.

Before we begin to discuss some very real HELPS available to the midlife male, take a few moments to read and properly digest the following aphorisms:

Grow old along with me! The best is yet to be—Robert Browning.

For age is opportunity no less than youth itself, though in another dress, and as the evening twilight fades away the sky is filled with stars, invisible by day.— Henry Wadsworth Longfellow.

Human beings can alter their lives by altering their attitudes of mind.—William James.

When one turns his attention inward he discovers a world of "inner space" which is as vast and as "real" as the external, physical world.—Willis Harmon.

As a man advances in life he gets what is better than admiration—judgment to estimate things at their own value.—Samuel Johnson.

There is more to life than increasing its speed.
—Mahatma Gandhi.

> Perhaps one can shed at this stage of life, as one sheds
> in beach-living, one's pride, one's false ambitions,
> one's mask, one's armor. Was that armor put on to
> protect one from the competitive world? If one ceases
> to compete does one need it? Perhaps one can, at last,
> in middle age, be completely one-self? What a liber-
> ation that would be!
> —Anne Morrow Lindbergh.
We know what we are, but know not what we may be.
> —William Shakespeare.

Recent studies at New York State University indicate that humor provides a very useful channel for covert communication on touchy subjects which might not otherwise be broached without jeopardizing a relationship.[1] A sense of humor developed and grown during a lifetime may help us mature and be able to actually laugh at some of our problems and foibles. If we can take ourselves less seriously, then perhaps the pain of midlife may be less intense. As Harry Truman once said: "The only things worth learning are the things you learn after you know it all."

Laughing at your midlife crisis may not make it go away, but it will give you a healthier perspective from which to effect a cure. As my father was fond of saying, when confronted by a seemingly insurmountable problem, "A hundred years from now I'll never know the difference." The midlife male may think he is experiencing a hundred years' worth of problems concentrated into a concoction too bitter to drink. But, the sooner he begins to work on his problems the sooner he will move through this traumatic experience and find a more settled time ahead.

The man in midlife feels like he is up to his armpits in quicksand. The more he struggles, the deeper he sinks. As he struggles to free himself from this seemingly bottomless pit he inevitably tries many things that fail to free him. Yet even the failures can become valuable experiences if, like Edison (after so many failures in his attempt to make a lightbulb) he can now say, "I now know a hundred ways *not* to make a lightbulb."

The first step toward overcoming the midlife crisis is for the man to keep himself in good health and well rested. Middle-aged men need to realize they are no longer twenty-five, they tire more quickly and take longer to recover, their stamina will not allow them to burn the candle at both ends. They need more vacation time to psychologically recuperate from the stress of their everyday lives. In addition to their regular vacation, they should build in long-weekend mini-vacations throughout the year to allow their bodies and minds to rest and rebuild.

David Morely in his book, *Halfway Up the Mountain* offers some sound advice to the struggling midlife male. Says he:

> To me, middle age is not the time when we should buckle up our belts, roll up our sleeves, and take another shot at youth. It's a time that cries out to man to consider his ultimate destiny, to think about the questions of whether his life has significance only in terms of his earthly experience. Or possibly it is a time to dare to believe that life—that brief journey (of no longer duration than the grass of the field, as the Psalmist tells us)—may be an infinitesimal part of a longer experience that exists beyond this present life, instead of seeing death as the gateway to an enigmatic abyss. . . .
>
> For a Christian, mid-life is a time when spiritual maturity can develop in its richest form, when the Person of Christ becomes a reality, the basis for a new and more meaningful relation with Him, which allows us to include Him in every innuendo of our lives. It's the time of life when the Christian, in ways that seem paradoxical to the world, becomes stronger, because he is increasingly aware of the strength of his Lord. It is a time when the fruits of the Spirit begin to flourish with the ripeness that is even evident to those who are not Christian. It's a time when the Christian can feel a freedom from the superficial stimuli that entrap the minds of most men—the greed, the egocentricity, the lust, the self-deception . . . lose their attractiveness.
>
> Christians do not escape the cruel process of mid-life,

but should be able to deal with this phase of their existence with a greater sense of challenge than people who are not Christians. . . . Mid-life, to a person whose perspectives are eternal, is a unique and exciting challenge, an exercising of his faith. To this kind of person, mid-life provides an opportunity for spiritual growth not before attainable. It is a time of fruition."[2]

But what if our spiritual life is at its lowest ebb? What if the above admonition toward spiritual maturity only makes us feel more guilty for our lack of control? What then? To those whose life is a spiritual vacuum, midlife can become an awesome shadow that chases away the dreams of youth and dashes the visions of the future. Like the author of Ecclesiastes such tend to cry out, "All is vanity and a striving after wind." Ecclesiastes 1:14, RSV. Therefore, it may be necessary for some to "lead up" to spiritual maturity. It may be a slow, painful process, requiring many other helpful proddings along the way. We have already mentioned rest and relaxation as vital in order to care for your midlife body, but we also need to develop a healthy self-image to care for our mental well-being.

Estimating our self-worth in the light of what God was willing to pay for our redemption by the sacrifice of His Son brings glory to God. If we belittle ourselves, we are in effect belittling God. To love yourself does not mean exaggerating who you are and overestimating your abilities. True self-love is not selfish or bragging. It means that you have made a proper evaluation of your strengths and weaknesses and that you accept yourself as you are *at this time*. You acknowledge God as the source of your strengths, and by His grace and power you continue working on your weaknesses. Loving yourself is not contrary to humility, rather it is true humility. It means you value who you are—emotionally, physically, and spiritually, because God considers you valuable. It means that you thank God for your positive attributes and dedicate them always to bringing glory and honor to Him. True self-love means you understand how much Jesus gave up for *you*. Since Jesus thought so highly of you that He gave His life in your place, how can you, the recipient of that love, belittle it by constantly being unhappy with your-self?

Many midlife males feel unhappy or empty, yet cannot seem to pinpoint the cause. They seem to be searching for meaning through something "out there." Actually they are looking in the wrong place. They are looking outside when the real solution has already been provided at the cross when they were saved from the ultimate penalty of sin.

True self-love is one way to happiness and final victory over the midlife crisis some individuals may have overlooked. Recognize that God will finish the good work He has started in you and that He accepts you right now, right where you are, just as you are.

If you are like the average midlife male, you spend a great deal of time criticizing yourself and displaying impatience with your lack of progress. A valid biblical principle is "*by beholding we become changed.*"

If we are constantly beholding our weaknesses, we become more and more like them. Unfortunately, self-criticism is socially acceptable and incorrectly labeled humility. We often say, "I really blew it this time!" But, each time we speak critically of ourselves, we strengthen the pathway toward that particular weakness. Perhaps, we think, if we criticize ourselves first, it won't hurt so bad if someone else notices our mistake. But, it would be much better to add another phrase to your vocabulary. Instead of saying, "I really blew it this time!" why not say, "It really isn't like me to make such a blunder. By God's grace I'll do better next time."

Real love begins with true self-love. Yes, there is a place for self-love. When Jesus said, "Love your neighbor as yourself," He was quite familiar with the true self-love principle and showed that He approved of it. Isn't it strange that self-love is usually set apart from love as a whole? As if to love every one else is good but to love oneself is somehow evil. This leads to a cycle all too familiar with most therapists and marital counselors.

Two people begin by loving each other. They mistakenly believe that love means to give without any thought of receiving.

As a result, they never really say what they need or expect from their marriage partner. They keep hoping their spouse will somehow read their minds and meet their needs without their verbal expression. These unmet needs begin to fester in both parties until gradually they ripen into resentment. This resentment is reflected in the male midlife crisis in all its ugliness and confusion.

Dr. Archibald Hart suggests three steps we can take to develop a healthy self-image:[3]

1. **Accept God's Unconditional Love:** Our basic worth must be founded outside of our human potential (or lack of it) in God's redemptive work on the cross and His subsequent call to all men to receive the salvation He provides.

2. **Develop a Realistic Self-Knowledge:** "Think your way to a sober estimate" (Romans 12:3, NEB), Paul tells us. We must develop a realistic awareness of who and what we are, and this is where pride differs from true self-esteem. Pride is always characterized by unrealistic self-knowledge.

3. **Completely Accept Yourself:** Thinking one's way through to a "sober estimate" involves more than just giving intellectual assent to a set of positive and negative qualities about yourself. Whether it is something you are dissatisfied with and can change—or whether it is something that is fixed and unchangeable—you must begin at the same point—*complete self-acceptance*. In saying this, I am not advocating that you be resigned to your inadequacies. This is simply a step in which you realistically recognize where you are *now*.

While you are in the process of accepting yourself, why not begin to fully accept the person you married? Why not begin to understand the difference between what you "expected" your married life to be, and the real, person-centered relationship of your marriage. Consider the following expectations versus reality:

A mother is never supposed to get tired or sick—but the woman you married does tire and does get sick.

A wife is always understanding and never lonely—but the woman you married sometimes gets impatient and does get lonely.

A wife is always supposed to be responsive to her husband and hence is always supposed to be ready to respond to his sexual advances with loving tenderness—but the woman you married doesn't always respond with alacrity to your expressions of love.

But what about the reverse side of the picture—as seen by a wife? Is it possible that she expected to find in you:

A husband who was self-confident and assertive in his work—but finds that the person she married is going through a crisis and that his confidence has been shaken and threatened?

A father who could be depended on, and who was happy to be the primary breadwinner and protector of his family—but instead falls short of her ideal—and just today was fired from his job?

A husband who she thought would always be self-assured and "in command"—but who instead gets tense and anxious, and sometimes even needs comfort and encouragement?

Every person who is married has a spouse who is the same, yet not the same, today as he or she was yesterday. A major problem solver in the midlife marriage is to recognize that an appropriate response today may be inappropriate tomorrow as both you and your spouse grow and change. Developing an honest and healthy self-image will allow you to share the real "you" with your spouse and not be afraid of condemnation or rejection.

Another "help" for the midlife male is to have a friend. But, how does one go about choosing a confidant? How do you locate someone you can trust with your fears and insecurities? How do you find someone who will validate your beliefs and provide a sounding board when you need to let off steam? How do you find someone (outside of your spouse) who will love you "warts and all?"

Unfortunately, friends are not found in your telephone book's "yellow pages." You must let more than your fingers do the walking to find a true friend. The amount of things you can share in common with another, your capacity to fulfill each other's needs, temperaments, interests, intelligence, values, abilities, etc., all come down to that mysterious item commonly known as "chemistry."

There are three types of relationships we all need in our lives. One is when a person ministers to us and we do not necessarily do anything in return. God falls into this category. A second type includes pastors, counselors, physicians, etc.—individuals who in the best relationships, build and minister to each other in a kind of give-and-take association. The third type are relationships in which you minister to someone else and perhaps never receive anything in return. In some instances your children fall in this category, along with the spiritually weak or otherwise needy individuals you might minister to.

While I cannot tell you who your friends should be and how you came to be friends, I can tell you what you can expect from true friends while you are going through your midlife crisis. A true friend will:

Be understanding

Not belittle your situation or actions

Have a listening ear

Keep your problems confidential

Offer unconditional acceptance

Keep in frequent contact

Probably have had similar troubles so he is more understanding

"A true friend unbosoms freely, advises justly, assists readily, adventures boldly, takes all patiently, defends courageously, and continues a friend unchangeable." —William Penn.

"In life you throw a ball. You hope it will reach a wall and bounce back so you can throw it again. You hope your friends will provide that wall."—Pablo Picasso.

"Friendship is the hardest thing in the world to explain. It's not something you learn in school. But if you haven't learned the meaning of friendship, you really haven't learned anything."—Muhammad Ali.

Employers are often a source of "help" during a midlife crisis. Unfortunately, unless you are employed by a company or someone that is "enlightened," employers are usually more interested in the production of things than the preservation of people. An understanding employer will realize that your condition is in all probability temporary and short term. That, when it is over, you will be more mature and be of greater value to the company.

During your midlife crisis you may not be doing your job as well as you should or could. A wise employer may change your job description or put you into another department with less stress, or he may encourage you to seek counseling. (Some employers even pay for such counseling for a valued employee.) In any case, talk with your employer before he talks to you. Try to explain to him what you are going through. *Ask* for his help and patience. More often than not, he will provide it.

Another source of "help" for the midlife male is his church family. Some individuals going through this period conclude that religion has nothing to offer them. Nothing could be farther from the truth—if the pastor is trained and has a living Christian experience. Using proper discretion, consult with your pastor. If it becomes obvious he doesn't possess the proper qualifications, find one who does. Many midlife males have found a new experience with their Lord during their midlife crisis.

Many churches offer seminars, retreats, and small discussion groups to help their members through this confusing experience in their lives. Church members who have a concern for those going through the midlife crisis should be aware of midlife symptoms and offer real support. This includes more than back-slapping and meaningless expressions of encouragement. All too often individuals going through this crisis have slipped quietly out the "back door" because no one really understood and offered true Christian friendship. So, perhaps the most productive role the church can take is to become aware and *care!*

Another source of "help" for the midlife male can be his children—if, while they were growing up, he established good rapport with them. Some men find real joy in sharing their concerns with their children during this period of their lives.

Jim Conway, a pastor who went through an intense midlife

crisis, wrote a book about his experience, *The Male Mid-Life Crisis*. In this book he tells about receiving a very special gift for Christmas from his children. He was in the midst of his midlife crisis when his three daughters presented him with a short essay they had collectively written.[4] Here is what they wrote:

"The Ship Builder"

Once there lived a man in a quaint harbor town who repaired ships. He was known by nearly everyone, because he was the most skilled craftsman for miles around. Often he would repair damaged boats for no charge at all. He worked on sailboats of all sizes and types. When a sailboat would become unseaworthy, it would be brought straight to him. Ships were brought that had been torn by bad weather, had collided with other ships, had been misused, or even boats that were never built properly in the first place. He would take each one and soon have it ready to sail again.

The man was a great artisan and had been in constant apprenticeship all of his life to the Master Craftsman. The Master Craftsman was a builder of ships; in fact, he was the most skilled builder ever to have lived. The Master Craftsman taught the man the art of repairing broken ships, and because they were such close friends, the Master Craftsman even taught him how to build his own ships.

The man always seemed to have dozens of damaged ships he was working on at once and more always waiting. Often the man would work years to rebuild a single ship, working day and night.

Many times, he would become discouraged, for he saw only broken ships. He longed to leap aboard a fine, new ship and sail toward the Morning Star. He longed to feel the free breeze at his face and the salt-foam about his feet.

The man's fame continued to grow and often he was called to other port cities to work. Everything he did flourished. Many other men became apprentices to him and his work increased. Through his work and teaching, more and more ships were repaired each year.

Now, although this man worked most of his life rebuilding ships, his greatest work was not the remaking of broken sailboats, but it was the building of three beautiful new ships. These were his greatest pride and showed all of his finest artisan craftsmanship, because into these three ships the man had put his life and love.

You can imagine what a tremendous lift this pastor received when reading this letter of love and affirmation from his three loving daughters. Children can be a tremendous help during the uncertainty and self-doubts of midlife.

Another source of "help" is *you!* I have already mentioned the importance of physical exercise in a previous chapter. Aerobics are especially beneficial to tone the body, clear the mind, and rejuvenate the emotions. Learn to do aerobics from a book, or join an aerobics exercise class and participate with a friend. You will find these exercises extremely helpful for your periods of depression.

You can also take on new challenges or hobbies. During my midlife crisis, my wife was constantly prodding me to finish my doctorate. In the process of researching and writing this book, I I did just that! Challenges can provide a new lease on life and give you renewed feelings of self-worth.

Perhaps you may feel your new challenge is a change of occupation. According to the statisticians, the present generation will make approximately three career (not just job) changes in their lifetime. In my father's day you were considered a "drifter" if you didn't stay with a single career twenty-five to thirty years or more. That has all changed in the faster-paced and more mobile society of today.

Another form of challenge is to launch a sharing group in your church. Learn to honestly share with other human beings, in a nonthreatening environment, what you—and they—are going through. Learn to share your real feelings. Sharing how you really feel in a small group (which you trust) may help you find new strength and affirmation for your life. In such a group you will have opportunities to minister as well as be ministered to.

Your midlife crisis can actually be turned to your advantage. It can become the renaissance of your life—a time when you reorganize your skills and abilities; a time when you put to use the wisdom and knowledge you have acquired during your former life; a time when you continue your education, launch into a new career, or retool your mind for greater achievements.

References

1. Sally Conway, p. 142.

2. Morely, pp. 10, 11.

3. Archibald D. Hart, *Feeling Free* (Old Tappan, N.J.: Fleming H. Revell Company, 1979), pp. 125-131.

4. Jim Conway, pp. 280, 281.

Is There Life After Midlife?

> Humpty-Dumpty sat on the wall,
>   Humpty-Dumpty had a great fall.
> All the king's horses
>   and all the king's men
> Couldn't put Humpty-Dumpty together again!

One successful midlife graduate with whom I am acquainted, commented as follows on this verse: "It's only a nursery rhyme, but I have to smile now. Humpty-Dumpty is together again. All the king's horses and all the king's men had nothing to do with his fall, of course; having gotten together again, I'm not the same Humpty. I'm a new man—more mature, more understanding, more sensitive."

Isn't it encouraging to know there really is a graduation day? There will come a time when you can look back on your midlife experience as a positive step in your maturing process. If the midlife crisis teaches you only one thing, let it be this lesson: In the midst of the midlife crisis, and at all other times in life as well, *You need Jesus!* A total surrender to Christ enables the midlife male to rise above his problems and look upon them objectively. A midlife male who has found Jesus in his life has also found value and worth in his life. As he recognizes that Jesus loves and cares for him, it becomes easier for him to accept and love himself. An early church father, Augustine, summed it up with these words, "Our spirits are restless until they find their rest in God."

The midlife crisis is a painful period that no one wishes to repeat. But it can be a productive experience if it forces us off the "island of self" into the mainstream of life. It can focus our attention on the true values of life. It fixes our concept of Christ's unconditional love as we experience it in all its wondrous glory in our lives.

Having passed through the experience, it helps us to empathize more fully with people portrayed in the Bible who were going through tough times. Perhaps we can even identify more compassionately with the midlife Pharisee who came to Jesus by night inquiring what he must do to be saved. See John 3. It was to this confused midlife male that Jesus revealed the true source of eternal assurance: "You must be born again!" It was to calm the inner turmoil he was experiencing in this midlife that Jesus plainly said to Nicodemus, "God so loved the world that he gave his only Son, that whoever believes in him should not perish but have eternal life. For God sent the Son into the world, not to condemn the world, but that the world might be saved through him." John 3:16, 17, RSV.

It was this same unconditional love that Jesus expressed so fully when He called an impulsive, uneducated, smelly, midlife fisherman named Peter to be His disciple. Peter, the aspiring water walker, the tempter who tried to prevent Jesus' Jerusalem mission, the ear-slashing hero who tried to redeem himself for falling asleep in Gethsemane, the dogmatic friend who vehemently swore he didn't even know Christ, the ministry dropout who went back to his old ways as soon as Christ left the scene. Yet, into this unpredictable, midlife man Jesus poured love, information, affirmation, rebuke, responsibility, assurance, and trust. As the Lover and Enabler, He saw the potential in this midlife fisherman. You can read the results in the first twelve chapters of the book of Acts.

In a similar way Jesus will pour out His unconditional love into your midlife madness until you too become a "new creation" in Him. It is important for us to remember that in order for Christians to realize the dynamics of the gospel in their lives, they must become both vulnerable and affirmative to those with whom we live. This may cost a great deal, and there may be failures, but we can expect these if we are to build deep and meaningful relationships. The more we surround ourselves with protective mechanisms, the more lonely and withdrawn we will become. We need to reach out and take the risks of relationships, just as Jesus lived and loved.

God's Word will provide "soul food" to heal our wounds and restore our sense of self-worth. But, no one can read that Word for you. No one can pray your prayers for you. Others may have you on their prayer list, but they cannot take your place before God. Search the Scriptures and begin to look for solutions to your problems. The Bible was written for people going through a midlife crisis. Notice the suffering, despair, blame, and final assurance presented by the song writer in Psalm 102, RSV:

Confusions and helplessness. "Hear my prayer, O Lord; let my cry come to thee! Do not hide thy face from me in the day of my distress! Incline thy ear to me; answer me speedily in the day when I call!" Verses 1, 2.

Realization of impending death. "My days pass away like smoke." Verse 3.

Poor health. "My bones burn like a furnace." Verse 3.

Intense emotional problems. "My heart is smitten like grass, and withered." Verse 4.

Loss of appetite. "I forget to eat my bread. Because of my loud groaning my bones cleave to my flesh." Verses 4, 5.

Loneliness. "I am like a vulture of the wilderness, like an owl of the waste places." Verse 6.

Sleeplessness. "I lie awake, I am like a lonely bird on the housetop." Verse 7.

Social and career enemies. "All the day my enemies taunt me, those who deride me use my name for a curse." Verse 8.

Loss of poise and self-confidence. "I eat ashes like bread, and mingle tears with my drink." Verse 9.

Blames God for his problems. "Because of thy indignation and anger; for thou hast taken me up and thrown me away." Verse 10.

Life has no lasting effects (futility). "My days are like an evening shadow; I wither away like grass." Verse 11.

Recognizes midlife crisis. "He has broken my strength in midcourse; he has shortened my days, 'O my God,' I say, 'take me not hence in the *midst of my days,* thou whose years endure throughout all generations!" Verses 23, 24, emphasis supplied.

Final dependence upon God. "The Lord will build up Zion, he will appear in his glory; he will regard the prayer of the destitute, and will not despise their supplication." Verses 16, 17.

Search the Word of God. Look for experiences similar to your own, and you will find solutions and salvation. In your search you may find the answers you are seeking and in the process find what is truly important in life. Sometimes, when we consider what is really important versus what is relatively important, we find that we have nothing about which to be depressed and much for which to give thanks.

> Christopher Wren, the architect who designed so many of the great churches of London, told of walking through the building site of St. Paul's Cathedral, asking the various workers what they were doing. One explained that he was doing carpentry work, another that he was laying bricks, still another that he was putting stained-glass windows into place, and a fourth claimed to be carving stone. As he left the cathedral, Wren came upon a man mixing mortar and asked him what he was doing. The mason, not recognizing the architect, proudly responded, 'Sir, I am building a great cathedral!' "[1]

In a similar way, the work of your midlife years extends far beyond the immediate horizons of this transitory stage in your life. You are in the process of building a "great cathedral" for God. Look past the mortar and bricks and concentrate on the part you play in relation to the overall beauty of the cathedral.

As you review your actions and reactions while struggling with your midlife crisis there are undoubtedly many accomplishments of which you can be proud. But this isn't all. Remember that your weaknesses can often be turned to advantage if you learn to understand them. All of us have blind spots, and becoming aware of the existence of a problem is the first step in solving it. If you did not previously realize that you had certain shortcomings, this is not at all surprising. But the important thing is to acknowledge your weaknesses and seek divine strength to overcome them. "God keeps faith and he will not allow you to be tested above your powers, but when the test comes he will at the same time provide a way out, by enabling you to sustain it." 1 Corinthians 10:13, NEB.

As one author has written, "Unfortunately it is the sad, battering experiences of life that tend to bring out the worst in one, that summon up anxiety, bitterness, envy, greed, jealousy, destructive cruelty and Old-Man-of-the-Sea dependency. These can be crippling to the personality if not recognized and held in check (it is too much to expect to uproot them)."[2]

Is it true that it is too much to expect to "uproot" weaknesses that control your life? I think not. By God's grace we can overcome our weaknesses.

Midlife can be a very positive time once we have learned to cope with who we are and where we are going in life. For the midlife male, "The flurry of youth is passed. His life begins to fall into step with reality. He sees that he can gain a measure of control. His tastes become more discriminating. He begins to enjoy the things that he has, rather than long for the things he cannot have. He begins to learn about patience and endurance. The need for immediate gratification has diminished because he has learned that sometime in life we have to wait and the time of waiting ought to provide knowledge that one could not get in any other way."[3]

The post midlife male, if he chooses, can be more optimistic about life in general than those who have not been through it. He can see that wisdom and experience are at least as valuable as physical strength and stamina. He puts his youth and impending old age in proper perspective. Instead of feeling competitive with younger men, he can enjoy passing on to others what he has learned. He knows his experience can help someone else build "on his shoulders." He chooses and keeps friends on the basis of mutual love and appreciation, rather than on how they can further his career. He begins to mellow and become a gentler person. As a husband he becomes more tender and understanding as well as a more thoughtful and sentimental lover. As one author so aptly put it, "On the pathway towards maturity, there comes a point when one can let go of his own egocentricity and become part of something bigger than his own self-gratifying interest."[4]

The Bible refers to it this way: "In all these things we are more than conquerors through him who loved us." Romans 8:37, NIV. The word *conqueror* suggests that there has been a battle or conflict. Conflict means there was pain and suffering. Jesus did not eliminate the battles of life. They still have to be fought. But the war has already been won through "him who loved us."

References

1. Anthony Campolo, Jr., *The Success Fantasy* (Wheaton, Ill: Victor Books, 1980), p. 81.

2. Conran, p. 20.

3. Morely, p. 27.

4. *Ibid.*, p. 37.

APPENDIX ONE
The Female in Midlife
Karen R. McMillan

People have heard so much about the male midlife crisis and how the wife can help her husband survive that they tend to forget that women also go through a similar stage. And woe be it unto you if you are going through your midlife at the same time your husband is going through his. If you are not, you are in a much better position to minister to him. And, ideally, when your time of need arises he will be strong enough to help you through yours.

Actually, women go through two special adjustment periods that could be equated to the male midlife. The first crisis usually occurs in the early thirties and is often referred to as the "quiet nest syndrome." It is the time when the children are all in school and the mother/wife has time alone for reflection. She may actually begin to feel worthless and that the world is indeed passing her by. She may even feel that she has not kept up with her husband, and certainly she has not lived up to her potential.

At this time some women actually have an "accidental" child in order to continue that feeling of usefulness she felt when the children were younger and needed her more. She may begin to feel a sense of aging. Her children begin to call her Mom instead of Mommy. Somehow the word Mom was always reserved for her own mother and makes her feel about the same age. She may slip quietly into a deep depression, and no matter what others tell her, cannot seem to come out of her pit of self-pity.

All of this is occurring at a time when her husband is deeply involved in establishing his career by putting in longer than normal hours to assure his success. Some feel that the woman who begins her career in the early years of marriage (or before) does not experience this transitional stage because she too is busy establishing a career. She has no "quiet nest syndrome" because she has never been home during the day to experience the feeling. But those who have chosen to make homemaking their career are far more likely to experience this crisis.

In her twenties a woman is usually at the peek of her physical beauty. As she slips into her thirties, she may begin to question her attractiveness to others. For a woman, the over-thirty hurdle can be as traumatic as the over-forty hurdle for a man.

One researcher observes that men are permitted two standards of physical attractiveness—the youth and the man. A man's desirability is enhanced by signs of aging and by his power, wealth, and achievement, which have increased with age. Women are permitted only one standard of attractiveness—beauty associated with youthfulness. So, you can see why it is easy for an aging woman to begin to hate herself.[1] Insofar as women are generally valued for beauty, and female beauty seems to be equated with youth, aging robs a woman of her main value and at the same time her self-esteem.

At this time in her life, needing to have her beauty reaffirmed, and possibly not getting that affirmation from her tired, overworked, ladder-climbing husband—some women seek an affair. She hopes, by having an affair, to eliminate two causes of her depression—boredom and the need of affirmation.

A sophisticated woman in her thirties usually has no problem at all catching the eye of a younger man in his twenties. It is a natural attraction that strokes both egos. His ego—because she is an experienced woman in the full bloom; hers—because he is young and proof that she can still attract a younger man.

She may also develop a "new look;" go on a strict diet-and-exercise program, purchase a new wardrobe, and have her hair done in a different style and color. In many respects she goes through the same trauma her husband will experience in another decade. Unfortunately, her husband may not realize what is happening and be no support for her during her crisis. However, having faced this experience at this stage of her life often equips her to better handle her husband's midlife crisis.

But it is the second crisis that occurs some fifteen years later that is especially devastating to some women—menopause. Throughout her adult life, a large part of her identity has been anchored in her relationship with other people—her husband, her children, her parents, and so on. Is it any wonder that she has an identity crisis? Who is she—apart from her relationships? In both of her midlife crises, the battle is a battle of the mind. What she thinks of herself. Her evaluation of her strengths and weaknesses. Her ability to contribute in a meaningful way to her family and her community or church.

Perhaps we should take a lesson from my husband's comments in this book and take a lighter look at the female midlife crisis before we examine it in any detail. With tongue-in-cheek and fingers crossed, here is the Female Midlife Entrance Exam:

— Have you noticed how much your old friends look like "old" friends?
— Does the expiration date on the film box bring tears to your eyes?
— Are you forever calling the family dog "Seymour" (which is your son's name)?
— Do hot flashes provide the newest warmth in your relationship?
— Has scanning menus in romantically lighted cafés become a squinting challenge?
— Have your arms become shorter than your eyesight?
— Is your favorite sex position the one which least hurts your back?
— Was your husband's last trip out of town viewed as a relief rather than an inconvenience?
— Do the wrinkles in your vinyl luggage match those on your face?
— Do your varicose veins remind you of a map of the U.S. interstate system?

In her book *Futures*, Shirley Conran offers these identifying characteristics of this dreaded phenomenon: "It's when you stop thinking that pensions are a joke. It's when you start wondering what exactly a face lift is (and how much it costs). It's when the problem of how to get the man you want turns into the problem of how to want the man you've got. . . . It's when you stop confidently expecting an improvement in your looks, income, home or work (whichever is the most important to you) and start vaguely worrying about decay, decrepitude, dependency or death (whichever you had previously thought about least)."[2]

As she looks at herself in a full-length mirror day after day and sees the ravages caused by the ruthless tooth of time, the midlife woman may simply give up and let herself go, telling herself it doesn't matter if she is overweight or out of fashion.— "Who can keep up with styles and hemlines anyway?" Or, she may go to the other extreme and spend half her time in a beauty parlor and a small fortune on creams, lotions, exercisers, facial saunas, hair tints, diet pills, bee pollen, and a new wardrobe for whatever size she happens to be at the moment.

While the Bible may remind us that the "outward appearance" is not the important thing, Christian writer Joyce Landorf reminds us that men certainly do look on the "outward appearance"—and that includes husbands.

At midlife your physical health and emotional well-being are greatly effected by your diet. What you eat not only affects your weight and figure, but also your energy, emotional resilience, and all other aspects of your physical and mental health. Your need for supplemental vitamins and minerals (such as calcium) increases greatly because of the stress your body undergoes during this time. My husband has to constantly remind me to eat the proper foods during my dieting phases. I will starve myself all day and then have a chocolate bar at night. That type of dieting is not only ineffective, but can actually be dangerous to your health.

There are a variety of weight-control programs available in almost every community. Avoid crash diets that do more harm than good. Learn a new lifestyle so you can maintain your proper body weight. Next time you lose weight by proper dieting, reward yourself with a new dress rather than a double chocolate malt.

You will also find that exercise is beneficial to your emotional and physical well-being during this crucial time in your life. One of the best ways to work out the frustrations of dealing with your midlife (or your husband's) crisis is to take a brisk walk. I happen to be a fast walker, and my husband has to jog to keep up with me. As a result he has begun jumping rope (without a rope! He says the rope slows him down) and leaves the walking to me. Being faithful about exercise and diet will not only improve your physical and emotional state, but will go a long way toward improving your self-image as well.

In her book *You and Your Husband's Mid-life Crisis*, Sally Conway makes the following observation: "An important consideration, especially at mid-life, is how your appearance affects your husband. Since he is going through a giant upheaval as he rethinks his values and commitments, he is probably looking at you with an evaluative eye. How does he think you look? Do you dress to suit him? Are you sexually appealing? What does he like or dislike about your figure?"[3] Even if your husband has already gone through his midlife crisis, these are good questions to ask yourself from time to time.

Now let's examine some of the more noticeable physical symptoms associated with the female menopause. Because of the numerous changes going on throughout her body, a woman can expect everything from headaches to hot flashes, to insomnia, to that "dragged-out" feeling, to loss of vaginal lubrication, to dry skin and wrinkles around the eyes. In addition she may find herself submerged in deep, dark periods of depression that make her (and everyone around her) miserable. Dr. James Dobson suggests that women experiencing emotional instability during this crisis period should seek out a doctor who will treat them properly and not attribute their symptoms to "something in her head." He warns that many doctors are still grossly uninformed with respect to the relationship between estrogen levels and emotional stability. (I can't help but wonder if male physicians would be more understanding if it was their body.) However, Dr. Dobson also warns that estrogen is not a miracle drug, nor is it a cure for all the emotional problems of meno-pause. But, studies clearly indicate that women who are nor-mally emotionally stable can suffer very real emotional prob-lems due to the lack of estrogen associated with menopause.

It is important to note that menopause does not diminish a woman's sex drive. Some women seem to phase out at this "convenient" time, if their previous sex life has been unsatis-factory. But the wife who rates her sex life as emotionally and physically enjoyable will take menopause in stride. As a matter of fact, with the danger of an unwanted pregnancy out of the way, she may find herself able to respond more fully than ever before. Ideally, any sexual problems that existed in the mar-riage were cared for during her husband's midlife crisis, so that it is not necessary to deal with them again.

I imagine that women going through their second midlife cri-sis will find it easier in the next generation because our atti-tudes are rapidly changing. Women who currently are in their mid-fifties have probably been taught that a woman is judged by how well she marries and the success her husband has had. If she married well, she was considered successful. The women's liberation movement has changed all that, and per-haps for the better, since it allows today's woman to have her own identity and find self-worth on a much broader spectrum than society previously allowed. However, for the woman work-ing in the home, it is a different story. In our mobile urban soci-ety, cut off from family roots and her husband's ladder-climbing, a woman may find that her only source of "positive strokes" is her husband and children. This can be devastating during the "quiet nest" or "empty nest" period.

Sally Conway reminds us, "Your identity needs to be drawn from the quality of person you are, wherever you are. True, you are known by what you do, but you should be known by your *being* while you are *doing*. You need to be flexible and realize that your roles may change, whether you are a wife, mother, or employee, but you are still the same person and you have a mission in life."[4]

Here is something else to consider: We live in a society (liber-ated or not) that basically judges a woman by her looks. It often doesn't matter how intelligent she is, how much money she makes, or how effectively she communicates. The bottom line (at least initially) seems to be her looks. The media tells us this is true, advertising reinforces this concept in our psyche, and our husband's casual interest in a "curvy" female drives the point home. Because of that mind-set in our society I will briefly cover the midlife woman and her body in appendix two.

References

1. Lillian E. Troll, Joan and Kenneth Israel, eds., *Looking Ahead: A Woman's Guide to the Problems and Joys of Growing Older*, (Englewood Cliffs, N.J.: Prentice-Hall, 1977), p. 90.

2. Conran, p. 1.

3. Sally Conway, p. 170.

4. *Ibid.*, p. 45.

APPENDIX TWO
A Beautiful Midlife
Karen R. McMillan

Studies in physical attractiveness show that people do, in fact, judge a book by its cover. This instant judging often has a dramatic effect on those being judged. The findings suggest that expectations based on physical attractiveness can become self-fulfilling prophecies that may strongly influence the course of a person's life. The studies show that people known to be physically attractive frequently are perceived by others as having warmth, poise, sensitivity, kindness, sincerity, and the potential for social, marital, and occupational success.

According to Dr. Ellen Berscheid, professor of psychology at the University of Minnesota, these beliefs about physically attractive people—and the preferential treatment they receive—can have lasting effects on an individual's personality, social life, marital experience, as well as educational and career opportunities. The importance of physical attractiveness is actually growing (not decreasing as some would hope) and will continue to grow in a predominantly mobile society.

Lest we think physical attractiveness is no longer important in our marriage after the first blush of romance has worn off, a recent survey of paired college students revealed, contrary to expectations, that as the number of dates increased, attractiveness became a more important factor in determining if the partner was liked. It continued to increase in importance ahead of other factors such as intelligence, social skills, and even personality.[1] This does not imply that physical attractiveness is the only factor in making a marriage successful. In fact, it may not even be a major factor. Nevertheless research indicates that it is definitely a major consideration in today's society.

Sometimes, we as Christians are caught in a "Catch-22" situation when it comes to outward adornment. How can we package the outer body attractively and still be a Christian inside? One Christian writer has resolved this conflict in her own life with this counsel:

> "What difference does outward adornment make? It matters much, because a woman's appearance, her grooming, and her size are indications of who controls her life—Jesus Christ or self. Ouch! That sounds harsh, but I am also talking about myself! The times I have let down on my appearance, or my weight has jumped, have been periods that have not been controlled by my Heavenly Father. It was during a time when a lack of self-discipline, or self-carelessness or self-pity took over.
>
> "Accept yourself just as you are and then proceed to ask God to help you change the things that can be changed. After your next bath, take a good look at yourself in the mirror and commit every roll and bulge to Jesus Christ. Ask for wisdom and discipline into bringing those bulges under control."[2]

If you or your husband are going through a midlife crisis it is especially important that you pay attention to your body. Using the old excuse, "If he really loves me he will accept me just as I am" is unrealistic and nothing more than a cop-out. I have seen too many women use that excuse until the midlife crisis cost them their husband. Then, wonder of wonders, they seem to find the incentive needed to get their physical body in shape in order to attract another husband. Why not use that same energy and incentive to salvage your present marriage? You need to ask yourself, "If I really loved my husband, wouldn't I do everything in my power, and in Heaven's power, to look as attractive as possible for my lover and best friend?"

Some Christian women feel that, most of all, they should not follow current fashion trends when it comes to dress. Somehow wearing clothes five or ten years out of style is more "godly" than the current fashion. Perhaps it is the same mentality that prevents us from reading and using a modern translation of the Bible. The interesting point is that five or ten years ago another group of concerned Christians considered those clothes "worldly."

There are many reasons for wearing current fashions that harmonize with Christian standards of modesty. Such apparel will make you feel good about yourself, while at the same time it avoids that "odd" look which attracts the wrong kind of attention. Such clothing can actually make you look and feel younger. Some people act as if it were "more spiritual" to look old and out of date. In fact, during this time when your husband may be struggling with being attracted to younger women, you are actually doing your marriage a favor by looking younger.

It certainly is possible to choose fashionable, young-looking clothes that are appropriate for you without becoming a fashion model. There is every reason not to wear matronly looking clothes when your husband is going through midlife. In addition, if you are wearing fashionable clothes, you will probably have more self-confidence and carry yourself with greater poise. When you feel better about yourself, you will feel deeper concern for others as well as less concern for self. Thus, rather than drawing your attention to yourself, being in style may actually free you from such unhealthy preoccupation and allow you to meet your husband's needs.

It goes without saying, of course, that it would be poor stewardship to get caught up in every whim of fashion. I would recommend that you choose classic styling that enables you to look fashionable for years. A basic suit can be updated easily (and inexpensively) with a new blouse, scarf, or some other inexpensive alternation.

Clothes, of course, cannot substitute for the inner self nor can it take the place of proper stewardship of your body, which the Bible says is the temple of the Holy Spirit. See 1 Corinthians 6:19. Most of us would consider worshiping God in a run-down church inappropriate, if we could afford to do better; yet some of us pay little attention to the decor of the "temple" in which God's Spirit dwells—our bodies.

"You need to strike a balance between making yourself physically attractive and spiritually vibrant. Keep your feet in the Scriptures and remember that you want your earthly temple to reflect the Lord. On the other hand, don't use spirituality as an excuse for being dumpy and drab."[3]

Gloria Heidi says women should avoid the "menopause bob." Oftentimes the menopause woman chooses a short hairstyle because hot flashes and her busy lifestyle make it difficult for her to care for longer, curlier hair. Forget about what is easiest and ask yourself (and a trusted beautician) which style looks the best on you. None of the current hairstyles (within reason) are really difficult to maintain, especially with all the helps and gadgets available in any department or drug store.

In order to be attractive, it is not necessary for you to follow the latest hair fad, and certainly it is not desirable to wear a style ten years behind the times. Most hair stylists will agree that hair style is an "illusion." In other words, properly done, it can, on the one hand convey the impression of energy, vitality, spontaneity, and sexiness, whereas, improperly done it can convey the impression of being matronly, dowdy, harsh, and severe. All this and more can be said through your hair style (or lack of it).

Whatever hair style you decide to use, it should be one that compliments *you*! Consider your facial shape, body size, hair texture, hair color, skin tone, and other factors when determining which style brings out the best in you. The current fad may make you look like a total flop!

Here is something else you should consider in deciding on your hair style. Choose a style that agrees with your husband's wishes and tastes. Ask yourself: How does he like my hair? What pleases him? If your primary objective is to dress to please the man you love, it goes without saying that that includes your hair style (again, within reason). However this should not be interpreted to mean that, since your husband liked you with long hair when you were in high school, that that is the way he will necessarily like to see you now. Furthermore it may be a good idea to bear in mind that, whenever you change hair styles, it may take your husband a week or two to "orient" himself to the new you. So, don't expect raving compliments when you come home from the styling salon with a new hairdo. The compliments will come later after he has adjusted to the change.

Perhaps the most difficult subject to approach in a Christian context is that of makeup. There are those who use it and those who abuse it. Often we equate the abuse with proper use and then "throw out the baby with the bath water." Some even say, "If God had meant for you to have bright red lips He would have made them that way." One could carry that same philosophy so far as to say, "If God had wanted you to have short finger nails, He wouldn't allow them to grow." Or, "If God had intended for us to wear clothes He would have created us fully clothed!"

I think we must recognize that over use of makeup distracts from God's creation. On the other hand, proper use of makeup can do wonders in covering up the blemishes caused by "sin." God did not create our first parents with imperfections. Eve had beautiful skin and needed no artificial help. But sin has wrought its damage to the human body. Is it wrong, therefore, for those of us who need it to use a little extra help in order to look "natural"? If the idea is not to attract attention to ourselves, and a blemish does just that, is it contrary to Christian principle to look our natural best?

It goes without saying that makeup used to excess and taking hours to apply is wrong. The same can be said about anything else that is good in itself but is carried to excess. Maximizing your good features and minimizing your poorer ones, however, is part of good stewardship. If you apply the same principle in the area of talents, you would do the things that you are most able to do well and not waste time doing those things for which you are not gifted. If we do not criticize people for doing what they are most gifted at doing, why should we criticize them for trying to appear as naturally attractive as possible?

You may be wondering about a certain Bible text that says, "Let not your adornment be external only—braiding the hair, and wearing gold jewelry, and putting on dresses; but let it be the hidden person of the heart, with the imperishable quality of a gentle and quiet spirit, which is precious in the sight of God." 1 Peter 3:3, 4, NASB. I asked my husband to help me with this text, and his first comment was, "This text is not saying that *all* outward adornment is wrong. If we were to apply it to all outward adornment, then the same logic would prevent women from also wearing dresses. I'm certain Peter didn't have in mind for women to walk around nude. No, I believe God inspired Peter to remind us to get our priorities straight and stop spending more time on our outward appearance than we do cultivating the inner spiritual being that God is preparing for heaven."

After hearing my husband's "male logic," I then did some research on my own and found that the examples Peter used of "braiding the hair, wearing gold jewelry, and putting on dresses" were typical practices in the Graeco-Roman world. A great deal of time was spent by the women creating fancy hair styles in which gold jewelry and expensive stones were actually braided into their hair. The dresses of that day were likewise made of costly silks and brocades. Not having our assembly lines of today, each dress was hand made and fitted to a specific woman. This took both a great deal of time and money.

What Peter was trying to say, as I understand it, is that the women he was addressing were spending too much time trying to improve their outward appearance while at the same time they were spending too little time cultivating the "inner woman." As my husband once said, they had their priorities mixed up. That doesn't mean that braiding hair or wearing modestly attractive dresses is necessarily wrong, but it may be wrong if it becomes the *only* priority in your life.

Isn't it permissible for beautiful souls to come in attractive containers? Are the only "good" Christians those who lack an attractive outer "temple"? I feel there is no excuse for packaging the Spirit of God in a shoddy exterior. Our body is the temple of the Holy Spirit, and shouldn't such a temple reflect God? When Solomon built a temple for God (see 1 Kings 5:2 to 6:38) he didn't use leftover scraps to build a dumpy hovel. Instead, he used the finest materials available, along with his most experienced craftsmen. It goes without saying that the outside of the temple was less important than the plan of salvation enacted on the inside. However, the outside also reflected God's glory and drew people toward the temple and what it really represented. In a similar manner, shouldn't the Christian likewise make the "temple" of the body as attractive as possible?

As one author so aptly put it, "A beautifully framed picture is one that does not draw attention to the frame, but rather the frame aids the viewer to center the attention on the picture itself. And so it is with us. Our frame should not detract from the real person inside. Instead, it should contribute to focusing the attention on the real person—the hidden, inner woman."[4]

Perhaps this poem by an unknown author can help us keep our body and midlife crisis in proper perspective:

> Curtains fresh and snowy crisp;
>   Hearthstone swept of every wisp;
> Mirror-like each pan and pot;
>   Muffins tender, steaming hot;
> Floors immaculate and shining—
>   Voice irascible or whining;
> Puckered brow and fretful lips;
>   Eyes that witness joy's eclipse;
> Color-blind to all but grey—
>   Pity that she can't one day
> Leave untidy some top shelf
>   While she renovates herself.

Happy Renovating!!

References

1. "Physical attractiveness: It does count for a lot, studies show," *Jacksonville Times-Union and Journal*, September 13, 1981.

2. LaHaye, p. 97.

3. Sally Conway, p. 165.

4. LaHaye, p. 99.

APPENDIX THREE
Dressing for Midlife Male Success
Leonard D. McMillan

Keep up to date: Do not expect your clothes to last indefinitely (you won't, so why should they?) nor stay in style forever. It is far better to buy fewer clothes at any one time and keep current, than to buy bargains that may be out of style before you buy them. One way to cut the high cost of clothing is to buy quality clothing—in better stores—on sale!

Classics are always in style: Some styles never go out of date. Look in a five-year-old catalog and you will see what I mean. It is always better to incline a little to the conservative side when shopping for quality clothing. But conservative doesn't have to be dull. A good wool tweed sportcoat may never go out of style, but a flashy leather jacket may be inappropriate next year.

Buy quality—not quantity: Find out which colors best suit your personality. Then reduce your wardrobe needs by determining which colors look best on you and buy only those items that coordinate with your basic colors. That way a gray suit can look sporty with a dark colored shirt and dressy with a white shirt and burgundy tie. Reversible vests and extra (different color) pants for a suit are not quality and should be avoided. Remember that a well-dressed man is still judged by his shirt and shoes. It may cost more to have less, but in the long run, you'll look and feel better.

Be colorful: Choose basic, strong, rich, colors for your suits such as navy blue, grey, or brown, and then compliment them with a quality white shirt and a subtle but colorful silk tie. Avoid the cream, beige, lilac, or dove grey as they make many faces look drawn, haggard, ill, or tired. At best, at least for most men, they make the man look like he is trying to keep up with the latest fashion—and failing! If you are partial to some brighter colors (red, orange, etc.) buy them in polo shirts and wear them where appropriate. Rich colors can work for you; drab colors do not.

Wear appropriate clothes: Many midlife males fall into the neck-chain and open-collar-to-waist syndrome. Not only does it look ridiculous for most occasions, but it is a flashing neon sign of midlife. Wear clothes that are appropriate for the occasion. When you are playing tennis, wear a nice tennis outfit; when walking the dog, wear a casual outfit; when chairing the board, an appropriate executive suit. Dress with care and neatness no matter what the occasion.

Buy the correct size: Just because you wore a size fifteen neck in your teens doesn't mean you should still wear one in your forties. Buy clothes that fit properly. It may cost a little more and involve more careful shopping at a quality men's store, but it will be worth it in the long run. Nothing is more obvious than a shirt collar that is too big or too small—shirt waistlines (with buttons straining) that are too small, or trousers that flap around the ankles and sag (like a sack of potatoes) in the seat.

Keep your clothes clean: Rotating your clothes—proper pressing—and drycleaning when needed will help you always look your best. I have a little personal habit that rotates my suits automatically as I wear them. Whenever I take off a suit I hang it on the right side of my closet and whenever I choose a suit it is always from the left side of the closet. This prevents me from wearing one suit too frequently and allows the wrinkles to "hang out" before it is worn again. Another item to watch carefully is your shoes. Keep them shined and new looking through proper maintenance.

Care for the foundation: It doesn't matter what clothes you wear, if your body is a "mess." The best clothes will never "make the man" if he is untidy or physically unattractive. It is important to keep the body in good shape and clean. A well-cut suit can mask some physical faults, but it cannot mask an unwashed body and the resulting odor. From haircut to finger nails the midlife male should be neat and clean in order to look and feel his best.